THE BRADBURY CHRONICLES

MORE WILDSIDE CLASSICS

THE BRADBURY CHRONCLES

by

GEORGE EDGAR SLUSSER

WILDSIDE PRESS

THE BRADBURY CHRONICLES

This edition published in 2006 by Wildside Press, LLC.
www.wildsidepress.com

As writer before the critics, Ray Bradbury has suffered a strange fate. All admit his excellence, and yet no one has really taken time to examine the exact nature and limits of his talent. Why is this so? The first writer of scientific fantasy to achieve general recognition, he is looked upon with a veneration that is not without ambiguity. Histories of SF, as a rule, extol him but avoid detailed analyses. Recently there have been articles, of the academic sort, which purport to deal in depth with his art. These tend to be close reading—the relation of theme to style in a given tale or series of tales. Sometimes the question of genre is discussed: is he fantasy or SF? Or someone may investigate religious strains in his stories. There have also been university dissertations on Bradbury, which seem to be only more elaborate versions of the same: we learn he writes well, discover formal complexity and examine patterns of imagery. But the writer is constantly treated as if he existed in a vacuum. The "safe" problems of style and form draw attention away from a much more central issue—literary context. Our of what specific literary currents has he written, and is he writing? Bradbury has been honored with a Vintage collection. In the introduction, however, the distinguished scholar Gilbert Highet is embarrassingly vague about the nature and sources of the work he presents: Bradbury writes fantasy (this is more respectable than SF), his ancestors are Hoffmann and Poe (aren't they everybody's?); he is an "original" talent, a "distinguished American author." But originality can only be measured in terms of a tradition. If this is, as Highet suggests, the American tradition, then what is Bradbury's place in it? This is a basic question, yet commentators avoid answering it. Are they afraid this uniqueness will pale when seen in a broader light? On the contrary, Bradbury gains in interest and scope when his work if firmly placed in the native heritage that nourishes and sustains it. It is the purpose of this study to do so.

First, however, Bradbury must be freed from the limits that now encumber him. In the absence of a true standard of judgment, false ones have flourished. Publishers and scholars alike are guilty in this regard. The former, to be sure, want to sell him to the SF market. On all the covers of the current Bantam paperback editions, Bradbury is hailed as "the world's greatest living science fiction writer." But this is to damn him with much praise, to grant international stature in a minor literary world. On the other hand, to label him a "popular writer", as recent academic studies have done, is just as surely to shelve him away. Bradbury's early stories, of course, were published in the SF pulps, and the later ones in the slicks—*Playboy, Post, Life*. But Hemingway also published in *Life*. And any number of now-established writers had what could be called "popular" beginnings. But they do not, as a rule, emerge from science fiction. Did a literary masterpiece; ever have a more unlucky beginning than *The Martian Chronicles*? The first paper edition displays a sleek rocket, and a line of close-cropped interplanetary fighting men rushing onto enemy soil, guns at ready. All this has absolutely nothing to do with the work inside, an incredible misrepresentation. The present Bantam series, many years later, is still adorned with traditional cataclysmic decor. Science fiction, in its worst image, sits on Bradbury like a stigma. With the academics he has gained a little ground, but hardly enough. Most of the serious articles are written, in periodicals like *English Journal*, primarily for school teachers. The implications are clear: Bradbury is good training for "serious" literature, excellent material for college preparatory students to cut their critical teeth on. Only when such artifical strictures fall can Bradbury ever hope to claim his rightful place in the sun. This study ignores them. The only limit placed on his art is that of American literary tradition itself.

The title of the sole full-length book written on Bradbury (ironically by a Spaniard) is *Humanista del Futuro*. But here, at once problems begin. Just what kind of "humanism" do we find in his work? And can we really locate his center of interest in the future? The contention here, to the contrary, is that he is not only an American writer, but a tenaciously regional one. Throughout his stories, the main thrust is never forward to Utopia, but backward, toward some golden age or American Eden, a place of childhood innocence, toward lost harmony with nature. Bradbury is not a speculative writer; he is not interested in envisioning new societies. He had his best chance with Mars, yet we learn next to nothing about this race in terms of institutions or historical evolution. And when he criticizes our society, it is because it has betrayed the land and culture it is rooted in. His stories are always anchored in a given soil, and his characters in a particular past. Not only is Bradbury no futurist; he is no abstract humanist either. His real task, simply stated, is that of portraitist—the chronicler of lives in isolation.

Many critics are unwilling to consider Bradbury a science fiction writer. His science is perfunctory, too unscientific; he does not labor to give us those elaborate extrapolated constructs which, in other writers, often leave little room for development of character. By the same token, we should not call him a fantasy writer either, for rarely in his stories does the machinery of fantasy exist for its own sake. True, Bradbury is master of the tale of uncanny surprise, in which the "normal" world is invaded, in the most startling ways, by hostile forces. This is the writer everybody remembers. And yet, as we shall see, even these early "classics" are often more than simple exercises in mood and form. Bradbury's later development confirms this—he rapidly shifts from situations to an emphasis on the all-too-human oddities of the people who experience them. The same is true of the mechanics of social protest. Bradbury airs his vision of social evil, but does not propose solutions. Gradually, in fact, as he becomes more and more fascinated with their products, he seems almost to accept the forces that shape human oddity and loneliness. All such machinery becomes a catalyst in his hands. The paraphernalia of SF is never more than a device which permits him to frame a series of human situations, and to extract from them his unique mixture of somber poetry and whimsical melancholy. The same holds for the conventions of fantasy: through these structures Bradbury aims at the mind of the fantasist himself, the strange dreamers of the world and their thwarted dreams.

The two poles of Bradbury's fictional universe are Mars and the American Midwest of his boyhood. These two disparate points on the map often seem the same place. In Green Town, Illinois, an individual explores his childhood; on Mars, an entire race searches for a new childhood. They bring with them their Midwestern artifacts, attempt to erect the old houses, to plant the old gardens and lawns on the new planet. But what of the other regions Bradbury has used as settings off and on throughout his career? These are all places he has known personally. There is the American Southwest, with which he became familiar in his Depression boyhood, as his father migrated back and forth across the land. There is Southern California, where the author has lived nearly all his life, although hardly at all fictionally. There is Mexico, where he has widely travelled, in person and in books. Finally, there is Ireland, where he lived briefly during the filming of *Moby Dick,* for which he wrote the screenplay.

Diversity of setting and differences of locale, can be quite deceptive in Bradbury. The particular regions are easily reduced to one archetypal region; beneath specific soils and pasts lie *the* soil, *the* past as he conceives them. Take for example Mexico and Ireland. There are contrasts in mood: the Irish stories tend to be humorous, the Mexican ones a somber baroque. The Dublin tales suggest Joyce, the Mexican, Katherine Anne Porter (whom Bradbury is known to have read). This, however, is veneer. Both Joyce and Porter, in their own distinct ways, recount with irony futile lives in a futile world. Bradbury is neither ironic, nor are his lives futile. His Irishmen and Mexicans, beneath it all, are very much alike—they are caricatures. On one hand, it is brogues and leprechauns; on the other, peasants speaking a Hispanese far worse than the Hemingway variety. In both spheres, Bradbury deals with the same social stratum: these are poor lands, life there is perpetual struggle. But this is as far as it goes. What difference is there, in these tales, between urban and rural poor? In both cases the poor are simply the innocent of heart. The stories are not specific pleas for change—solutions to the Irish or Mexican problem—but celebrations of the primitive power to abide. However "local" their manners, these men have in common their close contact with basic values—the land, friendship, family. They are, in general, victims of progress, and proof that humanity may yet survive its folly. In terms of literary models, these ethnics come closest to the heroes of Steinbeck's comedies of folk tenacity. But Bradbury's world lacks any hint of the biological determinism that darkens the latter's universe. Its composition, instead, is a strange blend of the sentimental and grotesque—a cross between Dickensian fantasy and the "human interest" story of O'Henry.

All places, in Bradbury, shrink ultimately to one place. His Southern California, for instance, is an oddly small town world. Even in the most recent tales, we have little or no sense of the megalopolis; if it were not for an occasional street name, we would never imagine this was Los Angeles. His Mexican-Americans exist in a stylized urban limbo of tenements, hot nights, and palm trees that could be anywhere and nowhere. When he portrays his Chicanos, he gives us characters of the same sort we find in the Bradbury heartland. Indeed, all his landscapes seem to press life into the same basic configuration. The Southwestern desert is a barren place, a ring of emptiness that forces people in on themselves and each other. His Mexican towns are described again and again as encircled and isolated in a vast land. This is, fundamentally, his Midwest: small towns, lost in the midst of prairie or forest, in their isolation becoming a prison, a hothouse world, a microcosm. In *Dandelion Wine*, the town and its situation become the symbol of human existence itself. Girded by woods, it is cleft by a dark ravine—the forces without cut through this universe of houses, sidewalks, and lawns.

Mars too, in this light, is only a transposition of this basic world. The Martians have disappeared, their planet is a waste land that weighs on its colonizers by its emptiness, driving them back on themselves and their past. Like the ravine, a Martian "spirit" runs through the lives, a subtle current that brings possibility of change and alteration. These men on Mars, each in his own heart, are forced to make a stand, less toward the planet (which is purposely faceless, absence rather than presence) than toward life in general. Man either resist or accepts, hold back or goes forward, vegetates or grows. Each must face the ring life has wound around his existence.

But with so much similarity underlying what at first seems so varied and diverse, how can we speak of development in Bradbury's art? There seem to be "periods" according to the type of story he writes. First, there is the "weird tale"; then, with the increasing use of SF trappings, the tale of social commentary, in which a projected future becomes a reflection on man's betrayal of the past; and finally, the "straight" character sketch, the unadorned chronicle of odd lives, in which the fantasy comes not from without, but flows from within a mind under scrutiny. *October Country* is replaced by *Fahrenheit 451*, and this in turn by *Dandelion Wine*.

But is there here, as some have seen, a concurrent movement from pessimism to optimism? In what sense is there passage from the autumn mood through a boy's magic summer to most recent promise of a new spring dawning? It is not by accident that the title of one of Bradbury's most recent collections, *I Sing The Body Electric!* (1969), alludes to Whitman; the volume ends with a poem very much in the Whitmanesque vein of poetic rapture—"Christus Apollo." In this poem, a new savior is born, man has awakened, has arisen—he will spread his seed of life throughout the waiting galaxies. One is reminded of these lines from Whiteman's "Passage to India": "Cut the hawsers - haul out - shake out every sail/Have we not stood here like trees in the ground long enough?" In this new Bradbury, there is the same messianic optimism. To proclaim it, however, he cuts the hawsers in quite a different way. The poetry he has adopted is unoriginal and bombastic; the prose he apparently has all but abandoned is his true literary foundation. Optimism is purchased at a high price—the falling off of his powers as artist. Indeed, the tree image is everywhere in Bradbury. Roots are essential to his world, and transplanting a hazardous activity, as his colonists on Mars discover. It is interesting too that this tree image is central to Sherwood Anderson's *Winesburg, Ohio*, Bradbury's prime model for his best collections of stories. Here, the "grotesques" who people these sketches of small town Midwestern life are compared to the gnarled apples the pickers have rejected: "Only the few know the sweetness of the twisted apples." Bradbury the chronicler, at the height of his art as a prose stylist, is among these few.

In a sense, then, Bradbury severs his roots when he sets aside the particular type of prose tale he perfected. The change is less one of basic philosophy than of artistic attitude. Bradbury trades a toughminded optimism, a sense of the bittersweet products of creation, for a facile one. His basic view of things, however, has hardly changed at all. Is not Bradbury's man, in the beginning as in the end, essentially innocent? Even in the earliest tales, whatever "evil" is present is not of human agency. The adversary is an extraterrestial, something that invades man from without, literally possessing him body and soul. If in the later works, man seems to spawn his own destruction, he does so not out of malice, but out of error. His cult of reason is a fatal misunderstanding of the processes of life; it stifles fantasy, and creates a cold, sterile world. In Bradbury's most recent tales, man simultaneously ceases to be invaded, and, miraculously, grows wiser. The machine, in itself, was never evil; the early Bradbury contains some marvelous evocation—who can forget the *boutique fantasque* of "There Will Come Soft Rains?" Man merely misused his machines; now he comes to use them well. From the start, Bradbury's creations, like Anderson's "grotesques," are firmly tied to the rhythms of nature, the round of seasons. Darkness was always there; now, it is simply recognized as a necessary part of the cycle of life: summers end, boys grow up, death must exist alongside youth and life. What seems to be development is really something more like clarification—the processes of life are rediscovered over and over as they gradually work clear from irrational fears and rational errors. Between an early dread of invasion, and his latest affirmation of the triumph of life, Bradbury reaches in his great middle works a delicate point of balance.

The design of this study is a simple one. There are two main parts. In the first, Bradbury's stories will be discussed as they evolve from earliest to latest. They will be divided into three "periods": "October Country," the first section, covers the fantasies of the early and middle Forties. "Vintage Stories" takes us from the first scientific decors and human interest tales of the late Forties through collections like *The Illus-*

trated Man (1951) and *The Golden Apples of the Sun* (1953), and includes the loose stories that group around the three centers of interest that are Bradbury's masterworks: *The Martian Chronicles* (1950), the unincorporated sketches of Mars; *Fahrenheit 451*, (1953), the tales of social commentary, and *Dandelion Wine* (1957), the various narratives of small town life and lives. Finally, "Machineries of Joy," Bradbury in the Sixties and Seventies, which includes the tales collected in his three most recent volumes: the title anthology, *I Sing the Body Electric!* and the most recent, *Long After Midnight* (1975). Bradbury is, first and foremost, a short story writer. In order that this not be forgotten, the first part provides tale-by-tale analysis. The object is to gather the loose ends, organize them around precise centers of interest, explore to what extent there is permanence in all this change, and demonstrate, perhaps, that, from one end of his career to the other, Bradbury is writing essentially the same kind of story.

The real development in Bradbury's art is not on the horizontal but the vertical plane. The second part of this study looks at three attempts to combine or expand single tales into larger, more complex literary structures: *Fahrenheit 451, Dandelion Wine,* and *The Martian Chronicles.* Discussion is purposely not chronological here. *Fahrenheit* is studied first for reasons other than its date of publication: in it, the temptation of the novel is laid to rest (*Something Wicked This Way Comes* is not, as we shall see, a novel in the same sense). And as fine a work as *Dandelion Wine* is, it nonetheless marks a lesser stage in Bradbury's art of the frame collection. *Martian Chronicles* is his classic, the work on which his reputation will ultimately rest. In *Dandelion*, the *Chronicles'* collective theme is abandoned for a narrower, personal one, its tautness and sparse economy of means give way to lusher, more ornate effects.

Ray Bradbury is a great fantasist and a superb entertainer. I hope to show that these qualities need not exclude artistic complexity. Every writer, of course, has his limits. Bradbury's, critics are fond of pointing out, are his decency and fair-mindedness—it leads to moral naivete, it is inviable in the labyrinthine modern world. But is the only literary response to the maze another maze? Bradbury has chosen to follow Thoreau's dictum and simplify. He seems to write about an America that no longer exists. Actually, he seeks to show us a deeper spiritual stratum that (he believes) always was and still is—energy, capacity for marvel, the desperate search for harmony with nature, incredible loneliness in the midst of its grandeur. The vision of a young land prematurely beset by ancient fears and dreams. Nevertheless, those who bemoan the fragility of tradition in America can take heart at the example of Bradbury: here is a science fiction writer whose stories all seem to prove that the soul is no traveller. The key to these mysteries of modern life is always the self-rooted in its native place. And the soul of his characters, whatever their nationality, is always an American soul. His rocket ship in a junkyard takes the most fabulous voyage ever imagined precisely because it never gets off the ground. Those who man it may have Italian names, but their experience is profoundly American.

THE OCTOBER COUNTRY

In his introduction to *The October Country*, Bradbury singles out a number of works as unique in his canon. This kind of story, he tells us, he wrote before his twenty-sixth birthday (1946), and rarely since. All these tales are purest fantasy. But it would be an error, for this or any other reason, to set them apart from the main body of the author's work, for they are seminal. If they display none of the SF trappings that were later to make Bradbury famous, they ask a question that is basic to this and all forms of modern fantasy: which mode of perception is superior—reason or imagination, cold logic or intuition? The October Country must be mapped. For it is here that Bradbury as he explores the implications of this question, shapes the forms and sets the directions for his mature fictional universe. Here, in these tales, is the matrix for scientific fantasies and "conventional" character studies alike, the model for future worlds as well as past.

The stories in question are varied. They can, however, be divided into two sorts: expansive and contractive. Bradbury's hero, in both, is a man of imagination and fantasy. In the expansive tale, though, the thrust of the action is outward. The hero sees, and on the strength of his vision tries to change the wide world around him. In the contractive tale, vision brings retreat within, creation of an alternate world inside mind or self. Bradbury's earliest stories, as a rule, are of the first sort. They are marked by the intrusion of some force—hostile and apparantly supernatural—into the narrow round of everyday existence. Vistas suddenly open out. The man of imagination, who sees this "unthinkable" peril, clashes with men of common sense or reason, who do not. Almost at once, however, tales of the second sort begin to appear. Here are bizarre ways of seeing things that are perfectly natural. The imagination before was a force with real heroic possibilities. These are truncated. Seeing differently now becomes a force that isolates, turning men in upon themselves.

The sense in which the first kind of tale is expansive must be clarified. Apparently, the main difference between the two types lies in the forces at work in them. In one, they seem unreal—a diabolical wind, a sinister crowd, vampires upstairs. In the other, they are natural—the tides of a lake, death. But how valid is this distinction? The French critic Tzvetan Todorov defines the "fantastic" genre in relation to the ideas of natural and supernatural. If in a story something happens that first seems unnatural, but is later explained in terms of current views of reality, then the tale is "uncanny." If the event cannot thus be explained, and new laws of nature must be formulated to account for it, the tale is "marvelous." The "fantastic" hovers in suspension between these two poles: is what is happening real or not? Very few if any of Bradbury's tales are "fantastic" in this sense. His expansive stories, moreover, are more "uncanny" than "marvelous." At first glance, the opposite seems true: the impossible happens; what invades the normal pattern of existence, apparently, is some alien enemy, or inexplicable, gratuitous evil. These forces prove to be profoundly natural once exposed. In each tale, there is always one who understands more than the rest. But he finds his answers not in new laws of nature, but in old ones like original sin, banished long ago by "progress." What seemed alien is, on the contrary, primal; the gratuitous has a cause—the human "sin" of knowledge, the fall of man and nature. These early works of Bradbury, like Todorov's "uncanny" mode, are essentially didactic: their purpose is to reset the boundaries of the natural world to include this "genetic" dimension. Once this is done, he abandons this machinery of intrusion. His stories henceforth are anchored wholly in nature.

Already in *The October Country,* Bradbury's view of the human condition has strong Calvinist overtones. In the earliest, expansive tales, the world, in a sense, is divided into elect and non-elect. Common men misunderstand both nature and their place in it. The hero sees. But vision, it seems, is both election and curse. The nature he perceives is depraved—some dark original sin has woven evil into its very fabric. It is as if he were destined, because he sees the true state of things and cannot accept it, to endure the most fearful punishments, not the least of which is unbearable isolation in his knowledge, solitary guilt. In these tales, there is the deed of imagination—the hero would fight evil, shape the world for the better according to his visions. He discovers not simply that this is impossible, but that such actions are the stuff of the malignancy he would destroy. His rebellion re-enacts the original revolt; in search of knowledge, he eats again of the forbidden fruit. Evil, in Bradbury's world, feeds and grows on such assertive intelligence. Works are of no avail; there remain only words—prayers, dreams, fantasies, the domains of the contractive tales. The withdrawn are also visited by "grace." But inner light brings its own endless struggle. These figures do not accept their world any more than the others. Their action, however, is to retreat, as if seeking some forgotten corner of an intolerable universe. If Bradbury's notion of things is Calvinist, it is, however, a Calvinism in abhorrence of itself. Only in the first stories do we have the unrelieved tragedy of visionary man, driven by human nature to search, yet punished for it. In later tales, though he retains this grim view of nature, Bradbury shows increasing sympathy with the products of its perversity.

Three stories of 1943—"The Wind," "The Crowd," and "The Scythe"—furnish excellent examples of Bradbury's early expansive mode. "The Wind" is one of the author's first professional sales (*Weird Tales,* March 1943). In a sense, though, it is archetypical. Its basic situation is that of Hoffman's "Sandman": everyday lives, devoid of imagination, are contrasted with the hero's lonely struggle against forces only he sees, and which seem supernatural. While Allin (whom we never see, only hear over the telephone) fights a losing battle with a wind that (he claims) has willed his destruction and stalks him, his friend Herb passes an evening at cards with wife and acquaintances. Here, as in Hoffman's tale, the housewife is the voice of reason: Allin's story of a valley of the winds is a "fable." his fears a "persecution complex." And what if his claims were true? Then he is only getting what he deserves: "You go poking around and first thing you know you get ideas. Winds start getting angry at you for intruding, and they follow you." "Reason" here is parochialism and egotism—the whole affair is distracting Herb from his family evening at home.

Ironically, however, her words, though spoken in ignorance, appear to be true—Allin has probed too deeply. What is this "wind" he has uncovered? To Allin, it is a force both sentient and diabolical, seemingly born of some dark primal act: "Something, a long time ago, gave it a start in the direction of life." Original sin? If so, this sin is re-enacted before our eyes. Allin delves into a mystery of nature, would alter it—he writes books telling man how to "defeat" the wind. It, in turn, is aware of him, pursues him. It does not simply kill him, however; it wants to "incorporate" him, take his mind. Explicitly, evil here is the aggregate of human intelligence and the suffering it causes: "That's what the wind is. It's a lot of people dead. The wind killed them, took their minds to give itself intelligence." If nature is malicious, man's fatal curiosity has made it so, and continues to do so. Significantly, the wind does not take just any mind. It avoids the ignorant (or randomly crushes them)—there is no wind around Herb's house. But it toys with Allin. While Herb plays cards, the wind plays a cruel game of hide and seek with his friend. What is dramatized here is intelligence begetting evil: the wind quite literally extracts its malice from the actions of one who, in vain, would outwit it one last time.

The story centers on Herb's card party for a reason. Because we do not witness Allin's struggle first-hand, we must use our own imagination to conceive it. In doing so, we give reality to this fantastic wind. But what if it is a figment? Our transition from fantasy to reality is paralleled by Herb's adventure. During the evening, his experience draws him from one world to the other. Tired of his wife's insensitivity, he renounces her and all like her—creatures so absorbed in their comfortable little lives they see nothing else. Going to the door, he is touched by a breeze from nowhere, hears what seems to be Allin's laugh stirring in the empty air. Is this a sign of election? Or is it a mocking curse? It is probably both. His imagination awakened, is he not the next victim of a cruel world order where the chosen few, seeking what they think a good, unknowingly feed the forces of evil?

The pattern of "The Crowd" is very similar. The hero, victim of a traffic accident, wonders where the crowd came from, how it got there so fast: "There was a vast wrongness to them. He couldn't put his finger on it. They were far worse than this machine-made thing that happened to him now." Again, a man has insight into what he believes an intelligent, evil force at work. By comparing photos of accidents over the years, he finds always the same faces—the ones he saw staring down at him. He prepares his evidence, but on the way to the police, another accident happens. The same crowd gathers, someone moves him, he dies.

We have the same question as the hero: what is this "crowd"? Simply thrill hunters "with a carnal lust for blood and morbidity"? The hero suspects them of worse—willful evil: "Vultures, hyenas or saints, I don't know what they...One of them shifted that woman's body today. They shouldn't have touched her. It killed her." His struggle to know continues right up to the end. As he lies on the pavement the second time, he sees them as "judges and jurors"; they are there to make sure "the right ones live and the right ones dies." But are they, like the antique fates, impersonal arbiters of destiny, executors of some neutral balance of things? Again the hero sees more: theirs is selective malice, they pervert the natural order. He knows his time is not up: had they not moved him, he would have lived. They did so purposely. They know he is "on to them" and must silence him; they take his brief-case with the evidence. This tale is perhaps less artful than "The Wind." But here no more than there are we meant to remain suspended. At this point, we ask if the hero's view of things is true, or merely a figment of his mind. Maybe he was moved by accident, maybe his time had come. We do not want to see this "crowd" as some inexplicable, alien evil among men. His final relevation, however, goes deeper. His last words are: "It - looks like I'll - be joining up with you." Our imagination is engaged; we must carry on the search. The crowd then, like the wind, feeds on human intelligence, incorporated it. After his first accident, the hero lived; he was "innocent." With his insight, his obsession, came the fall. The second time he seeks the crowd, and is taken. This crowd, it seems, is less a supernatural than a profoundly natural force: it looks down on the hero "like the large glowing leaves of bent-down trees," closes on him like the iris of an eye. This nature is depraved. And the cause of this depravity is not "carnal lust" so much as curiosity, the "sin" of knowledge.

The third story, "The Scythe," could be called a Calvinist allegory. An Okie on his way west with his starving family comes suddenly on an empty farm and a strange field of wheat. The former tenant lies dead inside; he bequeaths to him who comes a scythe and a task. An "inno-cent" Drew Erikson sets out to tend his field. Again, curiosity and ima-gination bring about a fall. Drew notices the odd patterns of the wheat: there are patches at all stages of growth; once cut, the ripe stalks rot, new shoots spring up. Then he begins to hear voices. One day, he thinks his mother has cried out from the cut grain. A telegram confirms his fears—his mother has died. In a flash, Drew sees the true nature of his job—he is the grim reaper. He cannot bear the responsibility; he condemns his actions as wrong, wants to leave. But he is unable to. His wife refuses: here is food, a roof over the head; his imaginings are silly. If there is something the matter with the field, call the "agriculture people." Drew is forced deeper into the torments of conscience. And even if metaphysical guilt can be stilled, personal grief cannot. He comes one day across the stalks that represent his wife and children, ripe for cutting. Knowledge leads to temptation; out of love for others he refuses to cut the stalks, breaking the implacable law of nature.

The implications of this situation are gruesome. The reaper here is no abstraction. He is a man, Anyman; he is chosen, but has no choice. Drew sets out on his road, driven by physical necessity, and it ends here, "as if there was no more use for it." In his testament, the old man makes it clear he is only "giver" of the scythe; the "ordainer" is absent. Nature compels him to wield this implement; put aside, the scythe cries to be taken up "as if a third arm had been cut off him." He would spare the stalks of wife and children only to find he cannot. Those ready to die must die. An irresistable force draws him out into the night field. Fire ravages the house. His family, who should have died in it, remain in limbo. He sees he must cut the stalks, but in doing it goes mad with grief, slashes down green wheat with the ripe; war and holocaust ensue. In the realm of nature, then, Drew has no freedom. He must cut the wheat, the dead going to their rest. What freedom he has is in the mind, and it is to one end alone—further perversion of something already perverted. He has no power to change the fundamental rhythms. By believing he can, he only makes things worse.

But why Drew? Is there any particular reason this man is chosen, and not another? In Calvinism, merit has nothing to do with election; indeed, Drew has no special merit. In Bradbury's version, however, the reason for choice seems, more than anything, to be cruelty itself. Because Drew has imagination, he is predestined to fall. We have here a terrifying extension of the Adamic sin. As with Adam, one man yields to the temptation of knowledge, and condemns all mankind to disorder and suffering. Yet the world of the wheat field is already one removed from paradise—there is death. Evil is not born of Drew's act, it predates it. Its roots, in fact, are in the awful machinery that places him in a situation without hope. How can we speak of free will when the seed of primal sin, the desire to know, is a necessary part of man's being—indeed the best part of the best men? A cruel world order lays on this chosen man a burden to heavy for him, torments him with the illusion that man alone can alter his lot, and holds him responsible for what ensues by making him, literally, the agent of destruction, the wielder of the mad scythe. This is a gloomy tale. The elect destroys as he is destroyed; the others look on, but cannot understand. As Drew mows away wildly, people stop their cars on the road to watch him; they can only wonder. In "The Scythe," perhaps, Bradbury exposes his cruellest view of man's condition, only to condemn it. The author does not, however, abandon it. If compassion for the victims grows in later tales, their world remains, basically, this same one. Dig a bit anywhere in Bradbury, and the old depravity reappears.

To be considered with these three tales from 1943 is a "shocker" written in 1946, "The Small Assassin." Again, something "impossible" is perceived: a mother gives birth to a child she claims has willfully tried to kill her. The doctor naturally sees this as something in her mind, the product of strain and trauma. She claims, however, that her child not only is fully aware, but hates those who brought it into the world. It is an enemy with a perfect alibi: it need only hide behind the accepted image of a baby—innocence, helplessness, ignorance of the ways of the world. Even from the womb it tried to kill her, she claims, because she "knew," had some intuition of its true nature. We recognize the pattern. There is however, one important difference: the evil invader is now openly and fundamentally part of the natural order, no strange crowd, but a baby. The implications are all the more frightening.

There are glimmerings of a social dimension in this story. It holds a key, perhaps, to later Bradbury tales, where society becomes increasingly important. The mother defends her view with all the thoroughness of scientific hypothesis. As she does so, she makes connections between heredity and what is commonly called "environment." Why shouldn't a child be born hating? He resents being thrust into a "lousy world." But in what sense is it "lousy?" Perhaps because there are crowds and confusion. the crowd, however, in the tale of that name, turns out to be more than a product of environmental error. Beneath a hostile environment, as we discover, lurks deeper ineradicable causes. Both the child and his world are offspring of some greater disorder. The infant trails no clouds of glory that will later be dispersed by the light of common day. Birth brings something quite different: babies are "elemental little brains, aswarm with racial memory, hatred and raw cruelty." The father is perhaps not wrong when he calls his child "Lucifer." What fell through intellectual pride is born "aware;" his evil is intellect without moral strictures. But how do such children become "normal" adults? The mother has an answer: "The world is evil...But laws protect us

from it. And when there aren't laws, then love does the protecting."
The Romantic vision of childhood innocence is replaced by something
very Hobbesian. Love is not a natural but a social impulsion—through it
man seeks to "protect" himself from elemental depravity. In this tale,
the skeptics are gradually converted to this alternate view of things.
The mother falls on the stairs and dies; the husband is convinced the
child set a trap. Later he too is killed; the doctor examines the evidence,
and is forced to admit it could not have been suicide. Only one other
being was present—the baby. The man of science goes to destroy him:
a scalpel brought him into the world, now it takes him out. Can this be
called an optimistic ending? Even if this agent of evil is done away with,
the cause of evil is not: in fact, one deed of violence merely begets
another.

"Skeleton" (1945) is an interesting variation on the now-familiar
pattern, and as such marks perhaps a turn in new directions. In this
tale, the hero is neither possessed nor invaded by strange forces from
without. He is obsessed, rather, with the divided nature of his own being. These lines of division are most unusual. We have a materialistic
twist on the old idea that the soul is prisoner to the body: here it is the
flesh that is captive of the skeleton inside. Again a man sees perversity
in nature and revolts; this time, however, the nature is his. To Harris,
the thing inside is "suspended like a delicate insect within a chrysalis,
waiting." Death will free it, liberating those dry bones. This insight
isolates the hero. His wife thinks he is overworked; medical science dis-
misses him as a hypochondriac. Only the queer "doctor" Munigant
sympathizes. But he is somehow too eager, ready to "treat" unwanted
bones anytime. Between these poles, Harris wages his oddly private
struggle with fallen nature.

Munigant tells the hero his problem is "psychological." He does not
mean, however, that it is a figment. In fact, the battle takes place literally inside Harris's head, where skull meets face. The narrative focus
shifts here, dwells on the eccentricities of this solitary, ingrown war.
The result is comedy. The hero refuses to eat, hoping thereby to starve
his other half ("no calcium for you, boy"). He loses weight, of course.
His wife like this new look—the strong, firm lines in his face. He re-
coils in horror: it's not me she likes, it's *him*! He encounters a fat man,
and is envious: his skeleton "could never fight clear of all that blubber."
For the first time in these stories, two "originals" meet. The fat man
has just as grim a view of the world: his "theory" merely comes at

things from the opposite direction. Where Harris would restrain what
lies inside, the fat man insulates against what lurks without: his fat
forms "a buffer epidermal state." For men of imagination, it seems,
there is no escape from the fault.

A question remains: who is Munigant? Harris at one point suspects it
was he who planted the fatal idea in his mind. But was he not obsessed
with his skeleton long before he visited the strange "healer"? Munigant's position is that of the old "doctor of souls" consulted *in extremis*.
Is he some devil hiding behind this mask? He does steal something from
Harris, after being invited inside. What he enters is, quite literally,
the physical body. He goes through the mouth and down the throat, not
to take the soul, but to devour the bones. This is, precisely, a world
where soul does not exist. And Munigant, more than anything perhaps,
is the symbol of its soullessness. He incarnates a basic principle of nature: what is already fallen can be further perverted by men's actions.
His "diagnosis" of the hero's problem is interesting: "Most difficult.
Something concerning an imbalance, an unsympathetic coordination
between soul, flesh and skeleton." Primal unit now shatters into three
parts, not two. Spirit, however, turns out to be absent; the battle rages,
grotesquely, between two forms of matter. Harris's malady is an excess
of materialist science: he probes his body like an "archeologist,"
classifies his bones, delves into the hidden corners of his anatomy.
In doing so, he gradually moves toward dislocation of self. His fate at
the hands of the fantastic bone-sucker only finalizes this dissolution.
Munigant, in fact, is less agent than instrument: he can only perform his
task when Harris chooses to let him do so. The hero's wife had humor-
ously cautioned him: "United you stand, divided you fall." She, like
the housewife in "The Wind," is probably unaware that there is already
division in the world. Ironically, though, she is right: better ignorance
than excess of knowledge. Deprived of his skeleton, Harris falls a second time. Fallen man can fall more. "Skeleton" shows that to explore
the microcosm can be as dangerous as actions in the greater world.
What is significant here, in terms of later stories, is this shift to the
world of the mind.

The tone of this tale disconcerts at first. We smile at the hero's tribu-
lations with his skeleton. We listen with amusement to the fat man talk-
ing of cultivating his intestines "as if they were thoroughbred dogs."
He is one of Bradbury's first great talkers, men who fill the voids of their
isolated lives with compulsive eloquence. In the end, however, we must

witness Harris's grisly fate—the boneless "jellyfish" on the floor calling his wife's name, Munigant outside playing "a little sad tune" on
his improvised bone flute to accompany her screams. This is a highly
stylized art of the grotesque. The moment of retribution has become a
set piece, a display of virtuosity. Later tales will merely drop it, as if
there were no longer desire or need to take things to such extremes. The
field of action moves away from these dreadful "punishments" toward
a middle ground more pathetic than tragic, more whimsical than grotesque. The accent will be on the bizarre investigations, the unusual
"philosophies" of such originals as appear in this story.

Two slightly later tales—"The Man Upstairs" (1947), and "The
Man Upstairs" (1947), and "The Emissary (1947)—still involve appar-
ent intrusion of the supernatural into normal everyday existence. But
the emphasis has clearly shifted. Before, an uncanny event erupted; the
hero staked his life on proving it both possible and natural. Now the uncanny remains hidden and buried. It functions beneath the organized
world of human society, or parallel to it. The question now is not,
"Is it supernatural or natural," but, "Who can see this alternate reality?" How can he reconcile it with the world of laws and love he must
live in? The heroes of both stories are young boys. Where the child before was an assassin, here he is seer, though far from blest. He may
perceive things adults do not, but his discoveries lead to actions that are
far from innocent.

"The Man Upstairs" centers on the problem of perception itself. The
"man" in question is a vampire, who takes a room in the Midwestern
boarding house of young Douglas's grandparents. To the adults, Mr.
Koberman is a normal human, if a bit odd. Douglas suspects he is more.
It is the boy who ultimately detects and dispatches this vampire. His
prime weapon is his childish capacity for fantasy. Not only does he believe vampires exist; he actually *sees* this one. Looking one day at the
boarder through the different colored panes of the stairwell window,
Douglas sees through his human facade, discovers alien forms within.
The window symbolizes the possibility of multiple realities—different
realms of vision—existing side by side: "Mr. Koberman, where do you
work at night...in a red world or a yellow world?" Through his under-
standing of the window, the boy reaches beyond his familiar world
into one that is non-human, primal. Koberman smashes these colored
panes to keep him out.

In killing the vampire, however, Douglas moves things the other way, "domesticates" the alien in the world of his elders. As he proceeds, he passes back and forth from one plane of reality to the other, stitching them together. The stitching image is in the text. Earlier, the boy had watched his grandma (in his eyes a "witch" performing her "miracles") void a chicken, stuff it, and sew it up. As the vampire lies in suspended animation, Douglas takes her knife and needle and performs the same operation on him. He takes his piggy bank from one world, sews its silver coins into a vampire's chest in another. The coroner jokes that this was "a wise investment." The deed, however, disconcerts both him and the other adults. If child is father to the man in this case, how innocent are his actions? Coolly he removes Koberman's guts—they have alien shapes. Earlier he had asked Grandma if the chicken guts were like his; she says yes. This is all the more frightening. We even sympathize with the vampire, reduced to just another experiment in the boy's unrestrained search for knowledge. Douglas gives a chilling appraisal of his work: "It's not nice, but it's interesting." Nor has he qualms either: "I don't see anything bad. I don't feel bad." Childish curiosity is seen in a gruesome light here. Perhaps it takes an amoral force to catch one. But next to the boy's natural actions, the horror of the vampire pales. Another form of lawless "science" dispatches the vampire only to reveal worse—itself. There is, however, a new situation in this story. Unconstrained intellect is at the crossroads. Douglas is no longer an "assassin"; and he is moving toward the adult world of law and love.

"The Emissary" is again a tale in which a child's curiosity leads to morbid discoveries. Young Martin is sick in bed in his small Midwestern town; Dog is his "emissary" to the autumn world outside—he brings back its smell and feel on his fur, a myriad of things for a boy's imagination to feed upon. But Dog is more; he is an explorer as well, he digs into everything: "How would I find out things if Dog didn't tell me?" To the adult, of course, this digging is a nuisance. Dog also brings people home to visit. One in particular is the young school teacher with the "autumn-colored hair." For Martin she possesses "the secret of signs, and could read and interpret Dog and the symbols she searched out and plucked forth from his coat with her miraculous fingers." Suddenly, she dies in this October season.

At this point, two worlds, two modes of vision, bifurcate. For adults, death is final. To Martin, however, "God's pretty silly." Why should they just lie there like that in the ground? In the parents' eyes, the girl

was Miss Haight the teacher, the boy's attachment to her simply stir-
rings of adolescent love. To Martin, she was much more. He, she, and
Dog formed a unified world of which she was the keystone: "this other-
half-of-autumn lady, who told him what was left untold by Dog." Theirs
was a game "with its special secrets and rules" from which parents
were excluded. His yearning, to them, seems merely boyish innocence.
And yet, perhaps, he has learned more of nature from her and Dog than
meets the eye. Is she some goddess of the seasons, gone to be the bride
of death? Does he summon her back? Dog is called by something, and
goes out again. Does Martin know what he is seeking? He fears Dog
is lost "to the wild throngings of civilization." When Dog finally
appears, he greets him with frenzied anticipation: "That was it, wasn't
it? wasn't it? wasn't it? wasn't it!" He had indeed dug deep this time:
from his fur falls cemetery earth. As painful footsteps approach the
room, Martin weighs the moral balance of things, his parents' view
against his: "Dog was a bad dog, digging where he shouldn't. Dog was
a good dog, always making friends. Dog loved people. Dog brought
them home." Ominously, the boy has not seen far enough either. Unity
is restored the only way possible in this fallen world—a corpse returns.
Whose emissary is Dog anyway? Through him the summoner is summoned. Martin may be ignorant, but he is not innocent. His too is a
quest for forbidden knowledge, its outcome a new perversion. Follow-
ing his alternate, lawless avenue of investigation, a boy plunges more
deeply into the grim ways of nature than his elders.

All these tales show a common purpose. They expand our vision of
things in certain ways—we go not so much beyond society as beneath
it. Man has erected his "civilization" over primeval nature. This pene-
trates the breaches in the system, and passes along its by-ways. In ac-
knowledging these intrusions, the hero does two things: he brushes
aside the artificial restrictions that blind man to his true condition, and
in doing so reveals these to be part of the same corrupt source. He chal-
lenges men's belief in "progress" and scientific rationalism, and we
discover that their roots lie in egotism, fear, and physical necessity.
What is more, these tales caution as well as instruct: man's imagination
brings about the evil it would abolish; there are limits to our powers. A-
longside these experiments, a counterpattern grows up—gradually it
adapts this particular view of nature in order to carve out of it a very
special fictional world. The fountainhead is another trio of stories,
this time from 1944—"There Was an Old Woman," "The Lake," and

"The Jar." Here "supernatural" intrusions are drastically modified, and often cease altogether: settings become pointedly real. Social conventions are neither flaunted nor surpassed; now they merely confine the man of imagination, isolating him. His actions are allowed no issue into a decisive event. Contact with primordial nature leads not to destruction, but to a twisting inward. This strain, in fact, finally absorbs the expansive tales. There, actions in the great world have given way to pursuit of alternate realms—instead of confronting social restrictions, the hero circumvents them, moving into a private sphere of action. Take away the ending of "Skeleton," let the corpse not appear in "The Emissary," and we have contractive tales. Characters remain sequestered in their alternate worlds, their experiences shelved as eccentricity.

The three tales of 1944 mark the extent of Bradbury's flirtation with the "fantastic." Outwardly the frame of "There Was An Old Woman" seems that of the expansive story. There is apparently a supernatural intrusion—a "dark young man" comes to take old Aunt Tildy off to death. She refuses, fights death—and seems to beat it even. The spirit left behind uses ruse and determination to reclaim her body from death and its minions—the unfeeling morticians. Even the skeptic embalmer is shaken in his narrow view of things.

The tone and emphasis of this story, however, bend this frame in a quite different direction, encapsulating the marvellous occurrence, and turning it to new uses. Indeed, there is less optimism here than meets the eye, or than the humor implies. One must complete the title. There was an old woman...who lived in what? In terms of her life, it is a tomb. As a result of her "philosophy" that death is "ridiculous," she retreats to her house, cutting off all relations with other humans because they "believe" in death. Her existence is twisted by this act of mind. Dying becomes a matter of belief, death in the guise of the "dark young man" just another suitor to be rejected for lack of intellectual rigor. Further perversion of the natural pattern ensues: she forces her spirit back into the empty body like "a butterfly trying to squirm back into a discarded husk of flinty chrysalis." There was an old woman... who lived in a corpse. The resurrected Tildy leaves the funeral wreath up over her door ("that's how her humor runs"). To visitors, her maiden fingers will expose her autopsy stitches. By the traditional laws of genre, we can call her fate comic. For a happy end, however, it is most gruesome in its implications.

The reader experiences a strange ambiguity here. Did Aunt Tildy really die? Did she return from the dead? Or is this all a dream? Her clock stops, continues to chime three. Here is the fact of her death. And here is her refusal to see it: "Shame, old clock. Have to get you fixed." The real situation in this story is not a mind at odds with death, but a voice. Though the tale is told in the third person, it is Tildy we hear. And death causes no break in this strange indirect monologue at all: this (if anything) transcends the grave. In the realm of fact, matters remain ominous—it is the living dead. Yet through her voice the dead remains very much alive. Against wreaths and stitches, we have her stubborn good humor: "Not bad sewin' for a man." Is there a supernatural happening here? We continue to hear the supremely natural voice of the old woman. But nature, as usual in Bradbury, is perverse and involuted. The voice does not cheat death. On the contrary, death enfolds and isolates it, permitting it to drone on in its harmless eccentricity.

In "The Lake," Bradbury comes about as close to Todorov's "fantastic" as he ever has. Here, as in "There Was," much of the ambiguity comes from the disparity between narrator's stance and the events narrated. This story is told in the first person. First we have the young boy on the threshhold of adolescence. Again, as with the old lady, there is "naivete" toward death. His childhood girl friend has drowned. He refuses fully to believe this, calling to her from the shore, but "the lake would not let her return." He builds half a castle in the sand, bidding her to come and complete it as was the ritual before. But water comes and washes it away. As in "The Emissary," a boy summons the dead—here, however, there is no answer. What was external is now internal. Instead of nature responding to the visionary, we have the faculty of vision interrogating itself: "You really expect answers to your calling when you are young. You feel that whatever you may think can be real. And sometimes maybe that is not so wrong." He hovers on the edge between two worlds.

The boy moves away, grows up, marries, and returns to the lake for his honeymoon. A body is found. Before he knows it is his lost friend, he has a premonition: "I held my breath and felt small, only twelve years old." The adult world is swept away. The body is so decomposed that he cannot possibly identify it, yet he *knows*. The thrust of this intuition is inward, away from reality, toward a realm of fantasy: "I have grown. But she has not changed...She still has golden hair. She will be forever young and I will love her forever." He walks down the beach, finds half a castle, footprints leading out of the water, returning: "This is where the guard found her, I said to myself." But is it? We are inside the mind of the narrator. Is what he thinks real actually here? The "wind" in the earlier tale attacked the protagonist; now the hero is brought to contemplate the meaning of the lake, and its relationship to the broader patterns of nature. The lake is less a thing than a rhythm of life. When the lifeguard sets the small body on the beach, "water whispered wet up around it and went back." Is it some supernatural lover claiming its bride? But the rhythm is the same as that of the footprints. The action of the water suggests to the hero further analogies: the tides take the other half of the castle; thus, he sees, time and the seasons take life, thus "all things crumble." Once again, something apparently supernatural is reintegrated with nature. This time, however, the process takes place within the hero's mind.

The natural pattern is grim; the private act perverts it further. The hero refuses to grow away from her whom death keeps ever young. The lake has taken both halves of the castle. But the unity the lake offers is to be had only in death. He does not commit suicide in the literal sense, but builds suicide in his mind. Drawn back toward this impossible past, he lets himself be cut off from present and future. His body walks away up the sand toward his wife. But she has become, to his spirit, a "strange person." As in "There Was," we have living death. Nature, however, does not do this to him; his own imagination, working on the rhythms of nature, twists and gnarls this life further.

The tone of "There Was" is whimsical, that of "The Lake" elegaic. The tone of the third story, "The Jar," is macabre. It is one of Bradbury's weirdest tales, and yet there is no supernatural element present. This parable deals with society, but in a unique way. Society is not, as in "The Wind," rejected outright; what is examined is the warped foundation of the social act itself. The jar is not a force that erupts amid conventional life, disrupting it. It does just the opposite—it polarizes; lonely men and women group around it, forming a society. What is in the jar? The story begins and ends with the same description: "It was just one of those things they keep in a jar in the tent of a sideshow on the outskirts of a little, drowsy town." In between, the contents have changed. But no one notices, no one wants to notice. There is a voice of reason in this tale, and no doubt it speaks the truth. Tom Carmody, the skeptic, says: "It's nothin'." The hero's sluttish wife learns from the carny boss who sold it to Charlie that it's a fake: "rubber, papier-mache, silk, cotton, boric acid." But Charlie and the others refuse to accept this. To old Granny Carnation, what is "really" there is not important. More essential is the mystery, for it gives all these lives a center to gather around: "When you said the same thing night after night in the deep summer, it always sounded different. The crickets changed it. The frogs changed it. The thing in the jar changed it." Under pressure of loneliness, the artificial thing, in the imaginations of these men, is elevated to a force of nature.

But if society is born here, it is based on no noble principles. Each sees in the jar only what he wants to see—the godhead, a dead child. It is the focal point of multiple egotism. The hero bought the jar for selfish reasons, to make himself the center of attention. Ironically, however, the new kingdom is not even his: the jar is the "emperor." And yet, no matter how perverse the foundation, the result is perhaps a good: "Thedy stood waiting for him to smash the jar. Instead, he petted...and gradually quieted himself over it. He thought of the long, good evenings in the past month...That, at least, was good, if nothing else." Inside this void of swamp and monotony and delusion, something comes to exist. To preserve it, he fills the jar with something "good" as well. Is it his wife's head? All who look continue to see what they want. The evenings around the jar go on. Here at last the subjective vision triumphs, fantasy winning out over cold logic. But the circumstances are more than grotesque. What "good" these poor mortals find is built upon the most twisted, ingrown actions imaginable.

A tale not in *The October Country,* but written in 1945, affirms the new direction Bradbury will take—not into the "marvelous" or the "uncanny," but into the fantasies of men, minds in jars seeking to people infinite space—"Invisible Boy." Here we have come full circle. There is nothing supernatural at all; no one is invisible. The emphasis is entirely on the human situation. The old "witch" merely weaves her fiction to be less lonely, fooling and not fooling herself. The boy too believes without believing. As a boy, it is his right to pretend, but also his advantage—his new "state" confers priviliges, lets him give free rein to boyish malice. The story is an interlude. Two lives meet and touch momentarily in this shared fantasy, then separate. The result is not tragedy, but pathos. The "invisible boy," in spite of all his cruelty, is nevertheless a real boy. When he goes, the woman withdraws: "...and over the fire at twilight she and Charlie sat, him so invisible, and her feeding him bacon he wouldn't take, so she ate it herself, and then fixed some magic and fell asleep with Charlie, made out of sticks and rags and pebbles, but still warm and her very own son, slumbering and nice in her shaking mother arms." "Magic" now has become the harmless defense of a lonely woman against reality.

THE VINTAGE BRADBURY

Bradbury's vintage period extends, approximately, from 1946 to 1955. Here, in a scant decade, there is the most intense creative activity. It is the period of *The Martian Chronicles* and *Fahrenheit 451*; much of *Dandelion Wine* is written at this time. These are perhaps Bradbury's masterworks. But Bradbury's art, if it is to be understood, should not be taken first at this level, but at the base. Each long work is either an expansion or compilation of short stories or sketches. Fundamentally, the vintage years are years of storytelling. Bradbury masters the short form.

Charting this period, however, is no easy task, especially in a limited space. There is a profusion of tales, and many are excellent in quality. Bradbury's production slows considerably after the later '50s. But during this vintage decade he is both prolific and fertile in invention. Classification seems necessary. There are three obvious thematic landscapes: outer space, future dystopia, and what can be called the "the odd corners" of the present or past. In the first category fall the tales dealing with rocket ships, space travel, extraterrestials, and Mars. The second includes tales of repressive future societies, projections of Bradbury's horror at aspects of our own. The third includes the many stories that recount human monstrosity, eccentricity, and isolation: we pass through a series of confined worlds back to Bradbury's small town Midwest. In general, stories of space travel dominate the late '40s, culminating in the *Martian Chronicles*. The majority of dystopian tales belong to the early '50s, the period of *Fahrenheit 451*. The third sort are found throughout the decade. They become more and more numerous as we move into the '50s, however, to form what appears as the Bradbury mainstream.

But how valid are such distinctions? What we have are not so much fixed structural patterns as highly flexible settings. Landscapes tend to mix and blend. Let a dead man awaken in some nightmare future: we find that he comes from our rural past. By the same token, time travellers from such future worlds land, not in urban today, but in small town yesterday. Is this a better world, or simply the one closest to our inescapable nature? Even space travel, paradoxically, carries us back to small town America, with its ingrown lives—this contrasts directly with the vast possibilities of the galaxies. In the background of the space tales, invariably, there is an atomic holocaust, or some intolerable utilitarian society on earth. Seeking to escape these aberrations of intellect, men are driven to further overreaching. Striving toward a future Mars, they are swept back relentlessly to their past, the fault that lies at the heart of nature, at the root of their American origins.

The three categories are little more than decor—beneath them some deeper dynamic is at work. Apparently, we can divide the stories of this period into two major modes—social commentary and human interest. Only loosely do these correspond to a public and a private dimension. It is better to see them as developing the expansive and contractive patterns of the early tales. Bradbury's dystopian works, in fact, are a modification of such early parables as "The Wind." These went beyond social issues to explore the metaphysical underpinnings of human existence. In the tales of future society, there is an exceptional individual, set apart by his vision. But his struggle is no longer directly with primal forces, but with this middle ground of man-made institutions. Before, it was an uncanny happening that disrupted the social fabric; now it is the "misfit" himself. In his eyes, the old nature, however somber, is still preferable to this new, rationalist perversion of things. He seeks to lead it back, or becomes its avenger. Bradbury uses space settings as well as a future earth for these dramas. Man's colonialist ventures are also a part of this collective folly.

These tales of social commentary can prove deceptive, however, or rather defective. They have no utopian side. There is no speculation on what society might be; the hero has no plans for change. The dissenting individual faces a monolith that nothing short of bomb or catastrophe can dent. His only alternative is the buried world. Completely isolated by society on one hand, he is driven back against the ancient patterns of nature. And yet, although suspended between nightmare and fallen Eden, this hero can only, in the long run, turn inward upon himself. The end product of the dystopian story is a twisted life. For a brief moment only, in *The Martian Chronicles*, does there seem to be any balance at all between social and human dimensions. And even here, the collective is really little more than a frame for the various individual dramas, men struggling with nature or their own natures. By the time of *Dandelion Wine*, we have shifted completely away from society on an interplanetary or even national scale, just as we have abandoned the broader elemental nature of the early tales. True, we have eccentric individual lives, and the town. But as public realm this latter is doubly circumscribed. It is isolated not only in its particular regional space, but in time as well. It is the past, and no general one either, but that confined in the memory of one person. Space and future both shrink to pinpoint private dreams and delusions, to lonely battles. At the heart of this vintage period is this slow triumph of contraction.

Bradbury's tales of rockets and outer space are quite varied in nature. Some of the earliest ones seem merely to transpose the old expansive tale into a new setting. Something happens, however. The technological possibilities of space travel free Bradbury from depending upon uncanny events alone to motivate a story. "Frost and Fire" (1945) is an interesting variation on the "radical memory" theme. In the course of interplanetary war, a group of men and women are stranded on a planet too near the sun. Days broil, and nights freeze; radiation has accelerated the growth process fearfully—man's life span is now eight days. The hero Sim is born "aware." But racial memory now has a natural cause: it compensates the swiftness of the metabolism. For most this is only a tool—they haven't time to learn otherwise. For Sim, however, it is a torment. He remembers another, slower world. He refuses this one, desires to escape, and thus sets himself apart. His peers blame the "Scientists" for their plight: their wars and experiments brought man here. Mankind has turned entirely to hedonism; wars are now fought for the best shelters, which yield an extra day or so of life. The swing is from one extreme to the other. Only Sim sees the connecting link—the "silver seed," the ship that lies just out of reach, the cause of their woes, and only hope for salvation. To break the deadlock, he must go alone. He reaches the ship, saves part of his people and they escape. This tale is too long, and much of the adventure is gratuitous. Yet its pattern is seminal. There is no progress in Bradbury's space. By overreaching, man brings himself to the most horrible predicaments. A hero like Sim does not "save" humanity so much as keep it limping along. Where will the ship go? Is the war over? Who won? Perhaps he flys from the frying pan into the fire.

There is, in "Zero Hour" (1947), what appears a supernatural occurrence—an invasion by Martians. Again, however, the scientific context makes this a possibility. We have an Earth of space travel and universal peace, balance of arms within, impregnable defenses without. The only breach in this antiseptic, rational world is the children's imagination. In a time when machines do everything for them, the adults envy their children's feverish tinkering. But they are still to "busy" to look under rosebushes or on lawns. Once again, imagination probes forgotten corners, releasing horrible forces. The story exemplifies Bradbury's particular kind of Manicheism: "Dark is horror, it is meant for contrast!" Ignored, this balance reasserts itself here, in awful ways.

In the tales of this period, the dark forces of fantasy do not always triumph. Cold, utilitarian reason is the victor in "The Exiles" (1949). Mars is the last refuge for spirits of fantasy authors banned on Earth as morbid or frivolous. A rocket expedition goes to Mars, manned by a new breed: "expensive, talented, well-oiled toys." The Exiles declare war, and try to reawaken fear and superstition in these antiseptic minds, of course, they fail. They learn the bitter truth: they cannot exist outside men's imaginations. If no one reads them, they vanish. The Earthmen hold a book burning. As these last copies go up in flames, the insubstantial pageant fades away, Oz crumbles, and Mars is empty.

"The Concrete Mixer" (1949) looks at this problem from a different angle. It is the satirical story of a Martian invasion. This time the Earthmen win, not by weapons or defenses, but by opening their doors. The world here is not a future one. We have, instead, Bradbury's vision of American life in the late '40s: fanatical religion, anti-communism, joyrides and auto wrecks, the crassest materialism. Ettil the Martian refuses to go to war. His reason: generations of Earth youth have been weaned on science fiction, stories where some young "Rick" single-handedly repels Martian invaders. "We never wrote stories of such a fantastic nature. Now...we attack, and we shall die." This time it is the Martians who are the book burining utilitarians; Ettil is one of the few who still believes in imagination. But not even he has enough to see what is in store. Ironically, he is dead wrong about Earth. Fantasists are a minority there too; in fact, no one reads at all any more. Forced to go, Ettil looks on as his fellow Martians are swallowed by the "concrete mixer"—fattened by the malt machines, lobotomized by the movies, reduced by chewing gum and depilatories. The Martians are truly conquered by a "Rick," but this one is no lantern-jawed hero, but a potbellied Babbitt, who turns a handsome profit from the invasion. Once again, the fall is re-enacted, but this time by aliens. Martian culture has grown arrogant, willing to abandon the old ways. A fatal ship from Earth comes to Mars; they copy it, get the idea to invade Earth in turn.

Thus is the seed of destruction sown: they will be conquered in the end, "the Blue Canal Night Club brought to Mars." If the planet were ever paradise, it is lost.

The concrete mixer is Bradbury's symbol for American materialism. A number of space tales from the late '40s and early '50s deal with this crushing, raping machine, and its futile destructive energy without purpose or soul. The moral of "The Man" (1949) is that wise men should not seek, but accept. A rocket ship lands on a planet where, an hour earlier, the "Man" had walked and healed. The Captain asks his lieutenant: "Why do we do it, Martin? This space travel, I mean. Always on the go. Always searching." Since reason destroyed belief, man can find no rest. The Captain, however, is a typical product of his age. Ironically, the chance to rest is here, before his very eyes. But he disbelieves: "Can't you see this is one of Burton's tricks, to fool these people...to establish his oil and mineral concerns under a religious guise!" It turns out not to be a trick; Burton died in space. The Captain, though weary, is driven on by his empty credo. He will go on and on, until he lays hand on Him. Martin asks: "Sir, when you find Him... what will you ask of Him?" Martin stays; the "Man" is still here to those willing to relax and believe.

"Here There Be Tygers" (1951) also deals with alternatives— aggressivity or acceptance. A rocket lands on a marvellous planet that fulfills man's every wish: "Suppose the purpose of this world is to make us happy?" One in the crew cannot accept this possibility—Chatterton the exploiter: "You have to beat a planet at its own game...Get in and rip it up!" The planet does not destroy him; he destroys himself with his restlessness. Just as medieval man peopled his maps fantastically with monsters—"here there be tygers"—so Chatterton fills this world with violent imaginings. Tigers appear where there were none, they devour him.

In both tales, the rationalist is a monomaniac who isolates and destroys himself. In each, one man stays behind. Is man at last learning to accept? In spite of this, Bradbury offers scant optimism here, and little promise of rest. The "Man" has in fact passed on. Is not the planet where Martin stays about to begin a cycle of events like that which had brought Earth to its present plight? And paradise in the second tale is lost. "If ever a planet was a woman, this is one." When the men leave, she acts like a woman scorned, throws a tantrum of fire and earthquakes. Never again will she accept them back. But why did they leave? Candide left Eldorado because he was bored. Not so these men. They are caught in an inextricable web of circumstance: "We've got our job to do. People invested in our ship. We owe it to them to go back." The social contract which regulates their fallen humanity bars them.

In many of Bradbury's tales, however, space and rockets merely provide a setting for more intimate dramas, studies in human isolation. In fact, one of the first rocket stories he published is such—"R is for Rocket" (1943). In the not-to-distant future a boy is chosen to be a member of the elite astronaut corps. The emphasis is not on outer space, but on the inner one of the boy's ordeal—he must leave behind his mother, and the best friend who was not chosen. Only a week before, he had played his childhood games, watching the rockets through the fence, dreaming. Now he passes that fence into adulthood. Private dreams issue into reality.

Generally, though, it is the other way around. Reality constricts, forcing men into a labyrinth of private fantasy and illusion. Space travel creates some odd situations. A typical example is "The Visitor" (1948). Saul Williams has an incurable and contagious disease. So he is sent to Mars to die. The disease itself further isolates these "exiles" from each other—they neither move nor talk, but only sleep and dream of death. Saul misses Earth and New York, but most of all he misses talk—he is an intellectual. One day a rocket brings Leonard Mark, a telepath with the power to conjure multidimensional dream images. Saul wishes he were in New York, and it springs up around him. He has a deeper wish, however: "Yes, why not? To sit and talk with Nietzsche in person, with Plato himself!" But others see this talent, and want it for themselves. Saul jealously seeks to hide the prize. Once again, a man pursues his dream of knowledge only to destroy it, to pervert things hopelessly. To kill Mark is "to kill Plato." This is what he causes to happen. He wrestles with the others, a stray bullet hits Mark, and the towers of illusion fall. Saul battles his solitude, only to have things get more and more twisted. Mark refuses to be "the intellectual bride of a man insane with loneliness." In so doing, he is pushed to worse extremes. He becomes a tyrant of illusion, "a god among children," ruling others with his powers for his own amusement. Saul courts illusion only to be most horribly deluded. Mark had enough visions for everybody. But herein lies the worst irony of all—his indifference. To him, Saul's need to talk with Plato is nothing special, just another commission. This man could never be bride or companion to Saul's spiritual yearnings. He too is empty.

On the surface, "The Rocket Man" (1951) is a family drama. Actually, it is a curious study in collective loneliness. Outer space drives a wedge between members of this family. This presence, however, is symbolic of the human condition itself. There is an archetypal quality about the figures here. The "rocket man" father is the essence of fallen man, caught between two worlds: "Every time I'm out there I think, 'If I ever get back to Earth I'll stay there.' But I go out, and I guess I'll always go out." The man's flesh is dark. But to his family he is light, his absence periods of darkness. The uniform too is black; to the son, however, it is resplendent. When the man first comes home, he digs feverishly in the garden, his face to the earth. But the ground he works is dark too, and the sky begins to seem bright by comparison. Seen from Earth, the stars are light; these are, however, but points in vast blackness. Space is a place of death, it is everywhere out there. But death is quick—this itself is a spot of light in darkness. The mother is caught in a similar dilemma. She cannot bear star light, yet is fatally attracted to her husband. She loves life, yet lives in death: "When he went off into space ten years ago, I said...'He's dead.' So think of him dead." Like an Earth goddess, she would hold him; she lets the grass luxuriate, and he must cut it. Yet out of this soil the alien sunflower he brought from Mars springs; she is forced to extirpate it. Her own son also betrays her; he cannot help her hold the father, because he too has succumbed to the fatal pull of space. These people are driven into silent, private worlds. The father neither talks of space nor brings things; the boy must steal his uniform and extract the dust of galaxies from it. The mother moves in a world of wordless ritual. Death comes on what, ironically, was to be his last voyage. His plunge into the sun perverts life for her at the source: "And the sun was big and fiery and merciless, and it was always in the sky." She shuts day out, lives enfolded in night. The boy looks on with detached fascination: he will go out.

"The Golden Apples of the Sun" (1953) is the story of a man's obsession with that sun. Names are singularly unimportant in Bradbury—frequently a character will have only a surname. Here a nameless Captain flies his rocket into the sun to take from it a cup of fire. The ship however has three names: *Copa de Oro, Prometheus,* and *Icarus.* Is this high epic adventure, a new Prometheus bringing fire a second time to spent humanity? Or is it a new fall? Indeed, the motive is vanity: "And besides, it's fun...there is no reason, really, except the pride and vanity of little insect men hoping to sting the lion and escape the maw." Is the old stigma finally relaxing its hold? True, this time man does not fall into the sun, but he takes away only a "beggar's cup." The ancestral patterns are reiterated here; in the Captain's poem, the sun is a "burning Tree," its golden apples "Wormed with man and gravity." What is interesting is that the task is done with pleasure: it's fun. Man seems to accept his limits (he is an "insect"), and even find comfort in those limits. Though there are no directions in space, the Captain insists on a south and a north: " 'North,' murmured the Captain. And they all smiled, as if a wind had come up suddenly in the middle of a hot afternoon."

In certain rocket tales, social commentary and private drama coexist. An example is "Pillar of Fire" (1948). This is the story of the last dead man in a world that has abolished graves, corpses, and darkness. In the incinerator, "everything that can't be used goes up like a matchstick." Is William Lantry's rising from the grave supernatural? It is, rather, a natural reaction to man's unnatural behavior—dark hate spawned to counterbalance this antiseptic world. He too is the product of a "racial memory": "In his grave the new violence of this future world had driven down and seeped into William Lantry." There is a public drama—Lantry declares "war" on mankind in the name of this nightside reality. This, however, merely serves to frame the private struggle—he is alone. His crusade fails because of his loneliness. He tries to summon the dead to life only to find that he is alone even among his own: "they did not know nor believe in walking once the heart had paused...They were deader than dead was." Even if he killed all mankind, he is told, he would still be all alone: "You're nothing but a moving hate." Pronounced "logically dead," he (like the writers in "The Exiles") can only vanish. A more ironically gruesome ending a- waits him however. "I am Edgar Allan Poe..." he tells the men, as they lock him in a golden box, shoving him in the incinerator: "We know, we understand." In this future, "Cask of Amontillado" cold logic builds its seamless wall brick by brick.

Bradbury's Martian tales are essentially regional stories. As such, they can be compared with those from the same period that use Mexico as a setting. Both share a central theme—acceptance. In Bradbury, geographical regions seem to have a will to uniqueness. They resist, passively and actively, man's attempts to level them. The foreigner cannot remain what he was elsewhere—he must adapt or be destroyed. The persistent theme in the *Chronicles* is adaptation: Mars permits it. Mexico is much different. Not only are Bradbury's Americans more unwilling to accept, but the place itself is fundamentally hostile. The land absorbs the intruders, but in violent, grisly ways.

"Dark They Were and Golden Eyed" (1949) is a Martian tale not included in the *Chronicles*. A family is isolated on Mars by atomic war. From the first, they feel alien: "The wind blew as if to flake away their identities." Literally, this is what happens. Contact with this new world alters them mentally and physically; by some form of osmotic memory the "old names" return. Bittering alone tries to resist, but this proves futile. Indeed, change is for the better: they now become a beautiful people in tune with a peaceful land. Marie in "The Next in Line" (1947) is also isolated by a wind: "Oh, what a lonely wind. Mexico's a strange land. All the jungles and deserts...and here and there a little town." The land absorbs her too. But instead of a beautiful woman, she becomes a frightful mummy in the catacombs—the next in line.

What a pity that the old Mexican, in "And the Rock Cried Out" (1953), never invented his fabulous machine "that would help every man, for an hour, be like any other man." In the *Chronicles*, the Martians possess such an empathy. They use it either to deceive and destroy, or in pathetic attempts to be adopted. In Mexico, division is absolute. Americans may struggle to accept. Marie wishes that she had "religion," that she could accept and abide. Her husband retorts: "The minute you get a religion you stop thinking." Thinking is perhaps the problem of these foreigners: the hero of "Rock" has been "thinking too goddamn much" for his own good. But what happens when he stops? This couple, stranded in the land by an atomic war that has reduced their dominant nation to rubble, is gradually stripped of all they own, and finally slaughtered.

The emphasis in an earlier story, "I See You Never" (1946), is on the total incompatibility of America and Mexico. Mr. Ramirez liked life in the USA, and worked hard. But as an illegal alien, he is deported to his Mexican village—he will return "never." Mrs. O'Brien, his landlady, remembers the Mexico she has seen: "The iron mountains...no cars, no buildings, nothing." Can the twain ever meet? Earthmen on Mars become Martians; Americans in Mexico become dead men.

There are surprisingly few pure tales of dystopian nightmare in Bradbury. The classic, of course, is "The Pedestrian" (1951). A man is arrested for the "asocial" crime of strolling the night streets in a city where people are shut in tomb houses, prisoners of the tube. He is arrested for not having a job (he is a writer in a world where no one reads), for not having a wife to give him an "alibi," for leaving his shutters open and his lights ablaze—a beacon of human warmth in metallic darkness. The Bradbury of this period has a particular horror of the automobile civilization: cars are scurrying "beetles," highways monstrous death lanes. Significantly, the pedestrian is interrogated and condemned by an empty police car. Bradbury's protest is Thoreau's: society occupies every minute of our day with useless tasks; we have no privacy, no time for wonder. More than the clock, Bradbury's symbol of this human bondage is the radio. His story "The Murderer" (1953) is about another asocial who goes around "killing" the wrist radios and Muzaks that enslave men's lives from dawn to dusk. Values are inverted. To destroy a radio is now a capital offense, for man cannot bear silence.

The other side of the coin is "The Smile" (1952). this dehumanizing "civilization" has led to an atomic holocaust. Mankind, bombed back to the middle ages, violently rejects the past they blame for their plight. "Festivals of Science" are held where cars are smashed with sledgehammers. A boy takes his place in line for another "festival"—men file past the *Mona Lisa* and spit on it. Permission is given the crowd to tear it to bits. The boy however is struck by its beauty. He fights to save a piece of it; in his hand is the famous "smile." One excess breeds another. But there is always the lonely act of protest. However grotesquely, the spot of light persists amid overwhelming darkness.

These stories of dystopia and apocalypse are particularly unstable. They absorb the weird tale, only to give way at once to character studies and human interest. "The Veldt" (1950) is a companion piece to "Zero hour." Here too is a world where parents have become superfluous. George Hadley's family is shepherded by their Happy Life Home—the mechanical house becomes mother, father, and nursemaid to the children. Again, it is the children who break through to that primeval nature the machine has shut out. The "nursery" is meant to give an illusory existence to the child's mental images. But real lions are willed into being—and their parents are eaten. Rebelling against their unnatural upbringing, the children tap the raw, elemental nature of the "small assassin." Here, however, the fault is clearly society's. In such a world, neither bonds of law nor of love can be formed.

In many cases, Bradbury's dystopia or atom war merely provide a framework for fundamentally human dramas. At the heart of catastrophe, isolated men find brief moments of fraternity, or carve out private worlds to replace the shattered macrocosm. "The Highway" (1950) is such a tale. A poor Mexican farmer looks on as cars flood north. The last one stops. Hernando learns from the Americans who ask for water that atomic destruction has come—it is the end of the world. He returns to his ancestral fields, to primitive life in the sun and rain: "What do they mean, 'the world'?" There is contrast, to be sure, a right and wrong way to live. The accent, however, is not on society, but on humanity. The Americans are grieved, and the Mexican offers human sympathy: "For the first time Hernando ran when a tourist asked; always before he had walked slower at such requests." Another example is "The Rocket" (1950). In this future world, the rich travel by rocket, and the poor stay home. An impoverished Italian junk dealer dreams of the stars. He buys an old demonstration rocket, makes it into an illusion machine, and takes his many children on a fabulous voyage through space that never leaves the ground. Imagination solves a very real problem here. The money he had would have paid one fare to Mars—but who is to go? Jealousies are avoided by taking them all. At the center of a world of social injustice, in the privacy of his own domain, a man finds an odd way of restoring balance.

Increasingly throughout this period, Bradbury develops the "contractive" character study that forms the nucleus of his work as writer. All these tales have present-day settings. The uncanny is gradually absorbed into the everyday, until it finally ceases to exist—we discover that purely human actions can be stranger. Three works from 1947 show how Bradbury varies the moods and forms of his stories from the start. "The Cistern" is a somber study in loneliness, of wasted life and its tortured dreams. Two spinsters sit embroidering in the dull light of a rainy afternoon. Anna has an odd idea: "Wouldn't you like to live in a cistern?" Her sister passes this off as "crazy." Gradually, though, the queer train of thought becomes ominous. Anna imagines an idyll in the cistern—but it is a vision of love in death: "It's a perfect kind of love, with no ego in it, only two bodies, moved by the water, which makes it clean and all right." She dreams alone, her hands coarse and clumsy, her hair graying, her once possible love with Frank destroyed by mutual rigidity and egotism. Only the cistern offers beauty and grace: "It takes death by drowning to make [a woman] most beautiful of all. Then all the stiffness is taken out of her.." She goes to join Frank in the cistern. This situation has strange Puritan overtones. Selfishness and awkwardness are products of the fall; fallen flesh cannot be reclaimed by acts, only by death, and the ultimate abdication of all will to act. Out of this ingrown process of mind deadly dreams are born.

"Uncle Einar" is completely different. It tells of the humorous, but very real, troubles of a fantasy creature who is incorporated into the family of man. Einar has huge green wings; he is a member of the supernatural "family" of "The Homecoming" (1946). Einar falls when he hits a high-tension wire: his night-flying apparatus is destroyed, grounding him. He meets a normal woman; she marries him, and they have normal children. The woman accepts the winged man partly out of harmless vanity: no one else has a husband quite like him. Her real reason, however, is deeper: "We're in our cocoons, all of us. See how ugly I am? But one day I'll break out, spread wings as fine and handsome as you." But Einar's new "cocoon" of human life begins to chafe. He yearns to fly. His old life of fantasy is gone: now he is good only for household chores, or taking the laundry for a spin on cold days. Yet from the depths of despair he rediscovers flight. His children would fly kites—he will be their kite, soaring openly every day of the year. This phoenix is reborn out of imagination. Not all solutions to the fall are macabre or destructive.

"Jack-in-the-Box" gives these same themes of death and rebirth a new twist. Edwin's father, presumably, was run down by an automobile. His mother has withdrawn into her house—it alone is the "Universe;" all around it lie the hostile forests and chaos. Pain, loneliness, and fear cause her to sequester her child, rearing him in the gospel of this father-become-"God," shaping him in His image. The outside world may be cruel, but this one is more unnatural yet, made of "Persian lawns," tricks and ruses to keep the boy ignorant of reality and death. Yet, the harder she tries to contain him in this artificial Eden, the more surely he falls. One day, he discovers a "forbidden" door: he climbs to the tower and sees beyond the trees. His is the fatal act of curiosity: "Now you've seen, and you'll want to see more." The seed of transgression lies deep within his nature. He identifies instinctively with the imprisoned jack-in-the-box: "It was like holding someone's heart in your hand. Edwin could not tell if the box pulsed or if his own blood beat against the lid." The mother grows fearful, accelerating his "birthdays"—the opening of the numbered rooms that will lead to his becoming Man of the House, Ruler of the Universe. But then she dies; has the futility of her task broken her heart? Edwin ignores her death—she is "sleeping." He wanders outside, and finds the jack he had thrown out the window the night before: it has sprung, arms aloft "in an eternal gesture of freedom." "The doll opened its arms toward the path that led off between the secret trees...but the path lay silent and the sun warmed Edwin...At last, he let go of the garden wall." Beyond Eden, Edwin discovers a death which is life. He jumps up and down touching things: "I'm dead, I'm dead, it's good to be dead!" But how free is the jack, a ludicrous puppet in its box? How free is this jack?

In "Powerhouse" (1948), the religious undercurrent resurfaces—it is the story of a conversion. An Arizona trapper's wife receives word her mother is dying. She and her husband ride to town. On the way, she falters: she wishes she had "religion." Never before had she needed it—but how can she face death? "Trapped" between stormy sky and desolate mountains, they take refuge in a powerhouse. Here there are no people, only dynamos. Amidst their throbbing, she has an epiphanic experience: "Her body lay, a lifeless reed...Her mind, in all its electric tensity, was flung about...down vast networks of powerhouse tributary." Machine does not drive man here. Rather, he interprets his creation through an act of imaginative vision, reintegrating it into the order of things. It becomes the link between him and nature: "The earth was suddenly more than many separate things, more than rocks, houses...Suddenly it all had one pattern encompassed and held by the pulsating electric web." The pulse is still that of life and death, but the accent is on the upbeat: "Whenever a light blinked out, life threw another switch." She carries the analogy further. She (as part of the whole) is no longer alone, and loneliness itself need not exist: "The light could be in any room, all that was needed was to touch the switch." We can change nothing: works are vain, life is balanced by death. We can only accept or reject: "Loneliness was a shutting of the eyes. Faith was a simple opening." But this is not true of just any moment; there is something here like an access of grace. On first entering the powerhouse, she sees only coils and centrifuges; now the machines stand "like saints and choruses." No one, not even her husband, could give her religion: "It's not a catching thing...someday you just relax. And there it is:" a secularized grace for this most unlikely of "churches." Curiously, Bradbury describes death in the same terms in "El Dia de Muerte" (1947). Young Raimundo stands "frozen and quiet" as a car bears down on him. Death, like faith, is a matter of relaxing and accepting.

A grimmer experience awaits the hero of "The Illustrated Man" (1950). William Philipppus Phelps is driven inexorably by a strange set of circumstances to the hut of the old tattoo artist "far out in the rolling Wisconsin country." Where did it all begin? he asks himself: "It had started with the arguments, and then the flesh, and then the pictures." A shrewish wife leads to junk food; fat and the loss of his job drive him to become the Illustrated Man.

The old woman sits unmoving in the center of her shack; all her senses are stitched except the mouth: "Come in, I'm lonely here!" The heroine of "Powerhouse" discovered that "being alone was not alone, except in the mind. You had all sorts of peekholes in your head." The old woman is, literally, the embodiment of Phelps's extreme loneliness—on her hand she wears his tattooed portrait. She gives this twisted life some bizarre "peekholes," adorns every inch of his monstrous body with monsters that are spawn of his own brain, images of ingrown jealousy, hate, and rage. She turns him inside out.

This modern Fate neither determines the future nor foretells it. She places on Phelps two pictures of things to come: "I put ink on your flesh and the sweat of you forms the rest of the picture, the Future—your sweat and your thought." Phelps unveils the first picture, only to be horrified. It is a window into self: he is in the act of killing his wife. Consciously, he refuses to admit that love in his heart has been bent to hate. But his body cannot lie: an embrace spurned becomes a murderous snap of the neck; the deed comes to pass. Man, then, makes his own destiny, and is responsible for it. Phelps tries to erase the first picture from his chest, but cannot—the forces have coalesced, the act is inexorable. The second picture, on his back, is still blank. It fills in after he has killed his wife, showing him being beaten to death under a crossroads lantern "where all the summer night seemed to gather." Phelps kills and is killed, pays for his act and yet is victim. His future is a product of his past in a deeper sense—it is rooted in his biological existence itself: sweat and thought. Is he not, in a sense, predestined? Bradbury's fascination with freaks and monsters is part of his curious Calvinist view of things. They seem "chosen" for some terrible destiny of which their monstrosity is symbol. Indeed, the more Phelps struggles to free himself, the more monstrous he becomes.

Loneliness and monstrosity continue to be central themes. "The Fog Horn" (1951) shows these are not reserved for man alone, but are woven into the general fabric of nature. In this tale, a prehistoric creature rises from the depths of the ocean to destroy a lighthouse whose fog horn has summoned it from eons of isolation—a false hope that one of its kind is still alive. This pathetic surge of love is twisted by cruel circumstances into its opposite: "That's life for you...Someone always waiting for someone who never comes home. Always someone loving something more than that thing loves them. And after a while you want to destroy whatever that thing is, so it can't hurt you no more." The monster never returns. Only the horn continues to call into emptiness—the symbol of existence on "this pitiful little planet."

Bradbury handles the pathos of loneliness in less gloomy ways. In fact, a story like "The Great Wide World Over There" (1952) is all the more poignant for its touch of whimsy. Cora and Tom are an aging couple who live in isolation in the Missouri mountains. He has no curiosity; for him, this small world is enough. She, though, is driven to know what goes on in the "great wide world." But their isolation is more than physical—she can neither read nor write, and she has never gotten a letter. The visit of nephew Benjy changes this: he will teach her how to write, and they will have a mailbox and letters. But to whom can she write? They take out magazine ads, Benjy sends out letters, and an avalanche of mail arrives: "Corn collector's catalogues, Magic List numbers, flea killer samples. The world filled up her letter box, and suddenly she was not alone or remote from people." But Benjy's visit is only a summer thing. During this time, she realizes, she hardly looked at his face at all, only his hand. More ironically, in her happy fixation, she never did learn to write. Letters continue to come after he goes— she can neither read them nor respond. Things slow to a trickle, and finally stop: "And in all the years that followed she never passed the fallen mailbox without stooping aimlessly to fumble inside and take her hand out with nothing in it before she wandered on again into the fields." Like many Bradbury characters, she lived happily "never" after. Cora has her magic summer—it is one moment of light in engulfing darkness.

"The Tombling Day" (1952) is a variation on "The Lake." Tombling Day is a day of moving graves—a road is to be built through the old cemetery. The coffin of William Simmons, Grandma Loblilly's suitor of sixty years ago, is unearthed. Miraculously, he has not changed: "I been cheated! Death kept him young forever. Look at me; did Life do so much?" When one of the men says: "There're compensations," he speaks true. Out of this saddest of improbabilities will come unimagined joy. The body in "The Lake" was decomposed. The hero resurrected it in his imagination, and in doing so bent his own life away from the world and the future back into the past—it was he who, morbidly, stayed "forever young." Here, the body is apparently preserved. Grandma takes it home to watch over it; as she does so, she undergoes the agonies of imagination. Is this the same Simmons? "She glanced again and again at his face. It became slowly familiar. That memory of him that she had torn apart and put together for sixty years faded to be replaced by the man she had *really* known. And he was *fine* to look upon." There is no refuge in illusions. She puts on old dresses, makes herself up, but to no avail: "No..There's nothing I can do to make me younger'n you." She is right, and she is wrong. As she looks on, the body begins to age—one hundred ten, one hundred twenty years, it crumbles to dust. Grotesquely, in her clothes of lost youth, she does a new dance of life: "I'm young! I'm eighty, but I'm younger'n *him*... I'm younger'n *all* the dead ones in the whole world!" At the extreme confines of loneliness, on the edge of the grave, hope unexpectedly flares out.

"Hail and Farewell" (1953) is also full of such strange twists. What would seem a blessing turns out to be a curse; yet out of this curse, in an unforeseen manner, a new blessing is born. Willie never grows up. To some, this might be ideal: "What a shame, that all these flowers have to be cut...How does it feel, Willie? How does it feel to be young forever?" But Willie must live in the normal world; and there the gift is a bane. He is condemned to move ever on from family to family. If his body does not grow, his mind does. He becomes practical: "There *was* work for me, after all. Making lonely people happy. Keeping myself busy. Playing forever." What results is a strangely warped situation. Willie does "good": he gets himself adopted by childless couples, stays until he must move on, bringing at least a summer of happiness. "Better to've had a son thirty-six months than none whatever." But this "good" springs from a curse and a compromise. In the light of common day, the joys of childhood become just another job, a living.

In this same vein, "And So Died Riabouchinska" (1953), is a strange and dismal tale. Hope to dispel loneliness arrives in the person of the beautiful ventriloquist's doll. Fabian, however, is an unusual Pygmalion: he has not created an ideal woman, but recreated a lost one of flesh and blood. Riabouchinska is born out of intolerable solitude. But this act is unnatural; love is twisted to sadism and violence—he ultimately must kill to protect his secret. The doll is said to be "the lovely part" of Fabian; actually, he has created a monster. Ria breaks away from her maker: "She's raised a wall in my head and lives there, ignoring me if I try to make her say improper things." Ultimately, she condemns him: "Because while I've lived with your weaknesses and I've lived with your lies, I can't live with something that kills...There's no way to go on from here." The irony is stunning. Fabian sought companionship, and is met with moral rejection. The "good" action, the "truth," brings unrelieved catastrophe: "She's gone...Will you help me find her? Riabouchinska slipped bonelessly from his limp hand, folded over and glided noiselessly down to lie upon the cold floor, her eyes closed, her mouth shut."

Of all Bradbury's studies of this misbegotten world and its tortured victims, "The Dwarf" (1954) is one of the darkest. The tale is an odd variation on the love triangle. A gnarled dwarf comes nightly to the gallery of mirrors to dance in secret before the glass that stretches his frame to normal size. Ralph, who runs the concession, gives Aimee a peek at this spectacle. Instead of laughing, she feels pity. She learns who the dwarf is—he writes detective stories by night in a lonely room. These provide a window into his feelings and frustrations—one is about a dwarf who finally kills a man who torments him. Aimee wants to buy him a mirror; then he will not have to leave his room and humiliate himself. Her infatuation drives Ralph to switch the mirrors in his concession. On his next trip, the dwarf sees himself hideously reduced, and shrieks. He runs away and steals a gun. Ralph turns to face his mirrors: "He scowled at the mirror. A horrid, ugly little man, two feet high, with a pale squashed face under an ancient straw hat, scowled back at him. Ralph stood there glaring at himself, his hands at his sides." Suspended in ambiguity, Ralph sees both his nemesis and the image of his own ugliness of soul. He is lost in a new gallery of mirrors, the convergence of his own actions and the dwarf's story—fiction emerges fatally into life, life fades into fiction. This story continues the awful irony of "Riabouchinska." Well-meaning actions precipitate confusion and chaos. Aimee would do good; Ralph is not malicious, only jealous. The dwarf is warped not only physically but psychologically—his parents sheltered him obsessively from the wide world only to die and leave him even more horribly alone in the end. "The Dwarf" is a compendium of Bradbury themes from his vintage period and remains one of the finest stories he has yet written.

THE MACHINERIES OF JOY

Dandelion Wine stands at a crossroads in Bradbury. Pouring into it are these vintage tales of private oddity and twisted lives. Developing through and out of it is a different kind of study—collective eccentricity. From a center in the strange individual, the queer action, the circle slowly widens outward. Communities form, often of the most unusual sort. But the dreamer and visionary are no longer invariably alone. Men now hope to piece together Babel, reuniting regions, climates, bloods. Or they dream of going back in time, repeating old actions and doing them right. The earlier grotesque, tragic or pathetic, is now tempered with humor. Irony smiles more than it grimaces. Emerging in the '50s, this sort of story dominates through the '60s. It still holds sway in Bradbury's latest collection, *Long After Midnight*.

In these tales, however, there is not so much a change of world view as a shift in attitude. They reflect a desire for reconciliation, the need for some form of peace and unity this side of death. One of the characters has this to say: "Somewhere did Blake not speak of the Machineries of Joy? That is, did not God promote environments, then intimidate those Natures by provoking the existence of flesh, toy men and women, such as are we all? And thus happily sent forth, at our best, with good grace and fine wit, on calm noons, in fair climes, are we not God's Machineries of Joy?" In earlier tales we have machineries of hate, pain, and torment. The Dwarf could be "played like an accordion." Fate plays cruelly with all these misshapen beings, living symbols of the curse of imagination.

Now Bradbury turns from these gloomy specimens, seeking the "calm noons" and "fair climes" in which men might become machineries of joy as well. Yet we do not escape the old world. Linked to the rhythms of mutability, these moments of happiness are unstable, and the community ephemeral. Nature is still fallen and divided. There are "environments"; men are set against them, and they are "intimidated" by his presence. Why the odd use of "provoke" for "create"? Man is a "toy." Is he not also the plaything of some darker destiny, a destiny this flash of joy momentarily illuminates? These are only islands of light, single moments of elation swallowed by darkness. Occasionally, in the earlier tales, we saw them emerge from the most unlikely situations—the old woman in her coffin, the community around the jar, Grandma Loblilly's dance of life-in-death. Bradbury now expands these instants, letting them blossom forth. In doing so, he walks a thin line. He maintains his balance in some of the tales; in others, he plunges into sentimentality.

"The Watchful Poker Chip of H. Matisse" (1954) is pivotal. It is the satirical story of George Garvey, a "terrifyingly ordinary man." In a sense, it recounts a fortunate fall. No one had ever noticed Garvey; his conversation was "mummified"; he was alone. One day, by an odd but not unhappy twist of things, a group of beatniks "discovers" this absolute mediocrity. They come to marvel and mock: and Garvey's world is suddenly peopled. Scales fall from his eyes: "I've always wanted to be gregarious, never had the chance." What awakens, ironically, is a sort of racial memory—he turns out to have "subconscious genius." He would keep his success. This demands "staying power" in ennui, so Garvey begins to play the old self to the hilt. In doing so, he discovers the instability of things. He actually converts his audience: the beats begin to dream of hot water, and to drink beer ("It's intellectual. What a shame so many idiots drink it"). When the fickle machinery of snobbery turns against him, his inner self performs a *tour de force* to hold its public. If only he would lose an eye, he thinks. No glass or patch for him. He would mail a poker chip to Matisse himself, and have him paint an eye on it. Lo, his eye falls out—the "subconscious" transforms the flesh to meet its needs. Out of this ordinary man emerges the consummate decadent, a monster with an artificial eye and finger, dreaming of limbs that spout liqueur. A lonely man's need for society has made him a freak. At first frightened, he soon is "secretly pleased." Happiness is born of the most grotesque circumstances: "Do you know? Sometimes that incredible Matisse poker chip seems to give out with a *monstrous* wink."

"Icarus Montgolfier Wright" (1956) is a simple tale of man's joyous anticipation of flight. A rocket pilot lies dreaming on the eve of countdown: Who am I? What is my name? He envisions himself part of a long line of human attempts to fly, from Wright through Montgolfier and his balloon, and back to Icarus himself. This is not, however, a paean to man's ability to conquer space. Actually, the dream is another example of racial memory—vision does not go forward to future triumph, but back to past failure, to roots in the fall. Daedalus warns his son: "Promise you'll not go high, Icarus. The sun or my son, the heat of one, the fever of the other, could melt these wings. Take care!" In spite of this, however, the emotional impulsion is forward. As the pilot's question is answered, three stones are reset in Babel: "Icarus Montgolfier Wright. Born: nine hundred years before Christ. Grammar school: Paris, 1783. High school, college: Kitty Hawk, 1903."

In "The Wonderful Ice Cream Suit" (1958), a garment transforms for an instant the drab lives of six unemployed Mexican-Americans. Each alone is too poor to buy the suit. But Gomez has an inspiration: six men of equal height and weight, pooling their resources, can purchase it. To break it in, each takes an hour's turn in the suit this wondrous first night. Their experiences are quasi-religious. One throws away his address book, thinking of fidelity, or even marriage. Another, the intellectual, loses his shyness, picturing himself moving among the rich businessmen like a white apparition, converting them: "My voice is very small, but it grows louder...I say, 'Friends. Do you know Carlyle's *Sartor Resartus*?' " Most of all, Martinez attracts the beautiful girl at the window who never noticed before. She is nearsighted, but "even the blind may see this suit." She puts on her glasses, and contact is made. Oddly, at this point he backs away from reality. In the lives of all these men, in fact, the suit becomes less a means than an end in itself. Gomez gives up his ticket to El Paso; he will not abscond with it. White cloth caught the girl's eye, but it is the whiteness of Martinez's teeth that holds her. She wants the man, he withdraws into the communal world of the suit: "I will need the suit for a little while..I am uncertain. I am fearful of many things. I am young." The men later go to the roof to sleep. Martinez ponders: "If we ever get rich...it'll be kind of sad. Then we'll all have suits. And there won't be no more nights like tonight. It'll break up the old gang." What does await these lives anyway? This is the high point. The suit has become the spot of light around which these uncertain existences huddle: "In darkness, with the others, he faced the middle of the roof and the dummy, which was the center of their lives."

In "A Medicine for Melancholy" (1959), the "sovereign remedy" is actually the common one of love. Young and fair Camillia Wilkes wastes away in 18th century London of a mysterious sickness. Learned physicians are confounded. She is carried into the streets—why not let the public diagnose her, since they could do no more harm? One passerby, a young dustman, suggests only the moon can restore her—leave her out overnight. She insists; that night the dustman visits her, she is cured. Unlike Bradbury's many tales of old maids, here is one where maidenhood is overcome. But is this cause for celebration? Her parents do not want to dance. The cure is at the same time a fall: "The name of the ailment is Camillia Wilkes," her young man tells her. Once again, we have a magic night; the dustman is transformed in moonlight into a handsome troubadour. But again, as with Martinez, the girl wants not dream but mortality. It is the dustman who attracts her: "His head bent closer. Thus sooted in shadow, she cried with joyous recognition to welcome her Dustman back." In spite of the light and airy mood of this piece, the pull toward darkness is there. If Bradbury's old maids resist death, does Camillia not embrace it? This tale, like "Tombling Day," ends with a dance. In the latter, life surges out of death. Here we simply have the opposite—this is the more "natural" way, perhaps, but equally mortal. Each woman is offered one moment.

"Death and the Maiden" (1960) is a reworking of "There Was an Old Woman." Death comes for Old Mam, barricaded in her house, half her years afraid of life, the other half of death. This time, however, the comer is no "dark young man": "He wore a suit like that snow which slides whispering in white linen off a winter roof to lay itself in folds on the sleeping earth." What he offers Mam is a melting away of winter, a second brief chance at spring—in a bottle is the first day and first night she turned eighteen. This old maid will become a maiden anew. The Old Woman lived in her coffin ever after; Mam makes a joyous end, throwing open her musty house. The course of her life remains twisted, she simply accepts it: "Strange...now, all of a sudden, twenty four hours, one day, traded for ten million billion years, sounds fair and good and right." Naturally, to become a maiden again is to fall: death would "sleep with her." At the beginning or at the end, there is still one marvelous day, no more. But the new mood prevails here. In earlier tales, death was cruel, life crueler. Now the Dustman is a gentle healer; and Death promises Mam that, when all is over, he will be kind.

With "The Machineries of Joy" (1960) begins a series of ethnic tales in which differences of blood or region are, in limited and often peculiar ways, reconciled. If these stories are optimistic, it is in an oddly negative sense. Man no longer seeks to change things—simply accepting them as they are is difficult enough. Fathers Brian and Vittorini are at odds. The reason is not politics or ecclesiastical opinion—Vittorini's passion for rockets and space is only a pretext. The real problem is blood, Irish temperament against Italian. The Pastor exhorts the Irish Father to open his mind: "Climb in the rocket and learn from it." Such a lesson, however, is too abstract. What really convinces is the Pastor himself—he is of Irish blood, but raised in California: "Well, they do say, don't they, that California is much...like Italy?" The two can co-exist. And for counterbalance, an Italian from Montreal will be summoned—hot blood from a cold region. "The world's played tricks with out flesh," mourns Father Brian. Only if we let it, is the reply. In the final scene the two men sit down before the television to watch the countdown at Canaveral. For the first time, Brian accepts these two horrors of modernity. In turn, the Italian admits the Pope never wrote an encyclical on space travel. The Irishman drinks lacrymae christi, the Italian Irish moss—"an Irish transfusion." Brian prays: "And help me, O Lord, to be as those children before the great night of time... And help me to walk forward, Lord, to light the next rocket Independence Night, and stand with the Latin father, my face suffused with that same look of the delight child in the face of the burning glories you put near our hand and bid us savor." To him these glories "near our hand" are still more important—his stand has not changed. But he now adjusts his world to admit the Italian, letting him share one of its privileged moments.

Of two Irish tales, "The Beggar on O'Connell Bridge" (1961) and "The Anthem Sprinters" (1963), the former is a darker vision, yet one which nonetheless ends with a breakdown of barriers, an act of empathy this time less racial than social. An American writer in Dublin is beset by beggars. Attracted and repelled by them, he is unable to refuse their demands. Out of what he calls a "strange perversity," however, he will not give handouts to one of them—the man who stands alone with dark glasses, hatless in the pouring rain, at the center of O'Connell Bridge. This beggar plays divinely; yet somehow he is too good. And why no hat? Everyone in Dublin, no matter how poor, has a hat. He is a rankling mystery. To accept the beggars, one must think of them as actors. "But what if it were true?" What if they had lived with misery so long that they had to play-act to survive? The American hesitates and ponders. Finally he buys a hat, but too late—the old man had jumped into the river the day before. On his last night in Dublin, he and the hotel manager discuss the beggars. What does the one mean who shouts:

"There's only a few of us left"? "Perhaps he means there aren't many 'human beings' left who look...Everyone busy, running here, jumping there, there's no time to study one another." But the narrator has studied—too much study was his error. The only way to know is to be. He wanders down into the street, divesting himself of clothes and money, and staring back at the warm, lighted hotel windows: "What's it like up there?..Who are all those people?..Do they even know I'm *here*?" All the poor of this land converge in the one beggar in the middle of the bridge. Behind his dark glasses lies the abyss. The narrator is helpless to change. He can only accept, or atone, rather, laying the guilt on his own flesh.

"The Anthem Sprinters" is a humorous treatment of the relationship between poverty and the Muse in Ireland. Again a strolling American writer is caught up in native life, this time as participant in the national sport of "anthem sprinting." For the Irish unemployed there are but two pastimes: pub and cinema. Rival teams of "sprinters" race to clear the theater before the national anthem sounds at the end of a film. The American is drawn into the contest when one of the runners is incapacitated by songs on the screen: "Sure, it's money runs the world...But it's music that holds down the friction." He sprints for Doone, and wins, only to discover he is alone: all the others have succumbed to the song as well. He hovers a moment between worlds, looking back at "the bright sane world of Grafton Street," then chooses to join the others: "Then, to the tune of 'The Lovely Isle of Innisfree,' I took off the cap and scarf, hid these laurels under a seat, and slowly, luxuriously, with all the time in the world, sat myself down..."

Bradbury has continued to write this same kind of tale in recent years. An example is "Have I Got a Chocolate Bar for You!" (1973). Two lonely men—an aging Irish priest and a Jewish boy addicted to chocolate—form an unlikely friendship in an unlikely place and manner. In the age of Clearasil and psychiatry, this lad finds his cure, of all places, in the old-fashioned confessional. The two men never see each other—there is only the smell of chocolate and its absence. But once again, the marvelous thing lasts only a summer. The boy leaves in autumn, returning many years later, and leaves a chocolate bar (blessed by the Pope) in the poorbox to tell his passing. By now this situation has become a stock exercise. The theme of the single moment, on the other hand, has become obsessive. Another Irish tale, "The Better Part of Wisdom" (1975), centers around a dying man's revelation of his one sublime ex-

perience—a wild, week-long friendship with a passing gypsy boy. He
tells the story to his grandson (himself presently living such a friendship) to warn him of the pain to come. The boy accepts. Bradbury's
world has not changed. This "one special life" has blurred all that
followed: "When often I cannot remember your dear grandmother's
face...why does his face come back?" But the treatment has become
increasingly nostalgic and sentimental. It is as if the story now exists
only evoke this moment—fiction has become elegy.

Another theme that has gradually become mired in sentimentality
is that of the writer. In earlier tales, Bradbury openly champions the
fantasists. But there is a reason: they are a necessary part of the balance—there must be darkness. His current attitude toward the writer
borders on naked adulation and wishful thinking. The classic model
here is "The Kilimanjaro Device" (1965). A man in a time machine returns to the past to reclaim Hemingway, and give him the "right"
death. This machine is powered by reading and love—by "remembering what his word did to us twenty years...ago." Poe was abandoned
by his readers. But Hemingway's fans pool their collective energy to
reach out and help him. This is neither science nor magic, but rather an
act of imagination that would suspend the laws of this world even if it
cannot alter them. The driver of the machine is so impregnated with
Hemingway that he begins to talk "in the rythym of his way of saying."
And what can be done about "wrong graves"? "Treat them as if they
didn't exist...And maybe they'll go away, like a bad dream." The fitting
end for the writer is found in his fiction: "We will put you up on that
same slope...on Kilimanjaro, near the leopard, and write your name and
under it say nobody knew what he was doing here so high, but here he
is." Here is a strange variation on the age-old desire to lift those who
have given us a better world out of this imperfect one. But now, instead
of a star in heaven or a prince in hell, the writer becomes a character
in his own hellish heaven.

"Device" remains a moving tribute. Later tales in this mode are less
successful. "The Parrot Who Met Papa" (1972) is a gossipy story—or
is it a takeoff on the style of Truman Capote ("Shelley Capon")? The
parrot to whom Hemingway supposedly dictated his last, never-written
novel is kidnapped. The hero Ray (an "altruist") saves the bird from
Capon and his commercial schemes. It is not this thinly veiled fantasy,
but the bird himself who is interesting. Another "Kilimanjaro machine," the parrot recites Hemingway in his voice. What moves us is

not so much the new novel but this resurrection of the old novelist himself. Again, a real past of creative power (Hemingway's language itself) is set against an empty present—the phony life and speech of this literary fagdom.

"Parrot" is tainted by the very effeteness Bradbury protests against. A later tale, "Forever and the Earth" (1975), leans toward the mawkish. Thomas Wolfe is plucked from the mouth of death by a time machine, and brought to a future world to write the great space novel. All the modern authors have failed—space is too big. Only a big man like Wolfe, with his childlike enthusiasm and imagination, can fill it. This he does admirably, pouring out ten thousand words a day. He writes that last great book; unfulfilled promise is fulfilled. But the book must wait in the future, while Wolfe goes back to his deathbed. The implications are clear. The future is hopelessly dependent on the past: a penchant that began in a tale like "To the Chicago Abyss" (1963) is now a landslide. Also, to help an artist even finish his work, we must go to most incredible extremes. All science and technology are at the service of this literary body snatching. Wolfe wonders as he dies: "Was it a dream? Perhaps. A good dream." In the old Bradbury, it might well have been so, and all the more poignant for it. But now there is no doubt—the moonflowers bloom on his grave. We also have the divided world of Bradbury's recent poems. Beneath this thin gloss of assertion lies the old universe, all the gloomier for this grotesque contrast.

Finally, there is "I Sing the Body Electric!" (1969). In its faults and strengths, this story is the epitome of Bradbury's late style. A modern Gepetto builds an "electric grandmother," and redeems both the machine and a family broken asunder by the death of a mother. This is a strange tale, rather long, but with few actual events. Of the three children, only Agatha will not accept "grandma." It takes an automobile accident to reconcile them: everyone, including "grandma," learns an unexpected lesson here. The story, in fact, is strongly didactic. Its center is no more the accident than the long discussion of machines and love that precedes it. The speeding car merely sets in motion the chain of ideas exposed here.

In terms of reconciliation, "I Sing" represents a far point in Bradbury. If Fantoccini cannot reverse the fall with his puppets, he does a better job of holding the line than Bradbury's other seekers after knowledge. "Grandma" is delivered in a helicopter that becomes an "Apollo machine." She is enclosed in a beautifully sculpted Egyptian sarcophagus: "Her hands were crossed upon her carved bosom and in one gold mitten she clenched a thonged whip for obedience, and in the other a fantastic ranuncula, which makes for obedience out of love, so the whip lies unused." She incarnates Bradbury's ideal society of law and love. How many children in his tales became monsters for lack of these? This family would have gone that way, had not "grandma" filled the void. She has the capacity to give equal attention to all: "Hers was a mask that was all mask but only one face for one person at a time." In this way no child "gets lost" as happens in large families—no lonely twisted lives are shaped. Furthermore, her hieroglyphs speak not of the past but of the future. Her sun is not fire of destruction, or place of overreaching fall, but rather "an illumination to tilt our shadows to better ends." Her first word was a laugh—not of mockery but acceptance: "It said the world was a wild place, strange, unbelieveable, absurd if you wish, but all in all, quite a place."

In the discussion on machines, what has been Bradbury's constant view comes clearly to light. If machines are evil, the blame is ours: "It's all in the way they are used." Fantoccini's are "compensating machines." They provide an example to man with his fatal emotions and instability: "Being mechanical, I cannot sin...cannot be greedy or jealous or mean or small." But they are not gods, they learn from man as well. "Grandma" saves Agatha from the car, but is hit herself. Unexpectedly, it is not the saving that unites them, but the fact that "grandma" is indestructible: Agatha didn't trust her because she feared she would die like mother. These machines, jokingly, call themselves "Pinocchios." To Tom the narrator, the joke is sad. He knows that, no matter how wise and good "grandma" grows, she will never have the gift of life. Agatha thinks otherwise: "You don't have to wait. You're alive. You've always been alive to us!" Earlier, "grandma" had defined love: "Maybe love is someone seeing and remembering handing us back to ourselves just a trifle better than we had dared to hope or dream." In the story, this process has worked both ways.

"I Sing" is a Bradbury microcosm. Here in miniature is his unique evocation of the child's worlds. Here is the magic childhood that effaces all else. The story is sentimental, but not bathetic. Bradbury has not bought back his fallen world with cheap tricks; death, loneliness, the ravages of time are all still there. In their midst, we too accept the wondrous machine. It is impossible to read this tale without tears welling up. But they are, to use Bradbury's words, special tears: "not tears that drown, but tears that wash clean.''

FAHRENHEIT 451

Fahrenheit 451 is an expansion of the 56-page novella "The Fireman.'' The latter is not a good story: it is the kind of Bradbury most readers never see. How did the author rework this material into a classic? *Fahrenheit* is two and a half times longer. Yet it has essentially the same number of episodes. "The Fireman" consists almost entirely of events and discussion; these are strung out in tedious fashion. Bradbury rearranges the original elements. As he does so, he tightens the story in order to expand it in new directions. *Fahrenheit* deepens the social and natural contexts. In this matrix, new intricacies of character, and more profound personal relationships, are shaped.

Both versions begin *in media res,* but in quite different ways. The novella opens in the firehouse. Montag is already asking questions: how would it feel to have firemen burning *our* houses and *our* books? The alarm follows—the old woman immolates herself. Here is Montag's visible moment of fall: "his hand closed like a trap" on a book. He goes home to his wife, begins to examine his life. We learn he has been taking books home all along. Bradbury must explain Montag's strange actions: the firehouse, the books. To offset a clumsy beginning, he resorts to clumsier flashbacks. Here Clarisse comes in. Perhaps the people moving in next door had been the start of his new awareness: "One night (it was so long ago) he had gone out for a walk.."

The first scene of *Fahrenheit* is his meeting with Clarisse. A man comes home from a routine day, and confronts the unusual. Confused, he passes on to his house, and finds his wife dying of an overdose of sedatives. In "Fireman," this was a remembered detail. It becomes a striking scene: two macabre medics come with their "electric-eyed snake" and pump her out. Montag is stunned: "Strangers...take your blood. Who *were* those men?" Questions are yanked from him by these extraordinary happenings. Now the flow of time loosens. There is the first scene at the firehouse, and interludes with Clarisse. Suddenly she is there no more. Time contracts. We have the alarm—the old woman burns. Once again, Montag is driven; he seizes the book, going home to collapse. If he rebels, it is passively, stalling the world as he gropes for answers. This rhythm of constriction and release continues all across the narrative. The changes in the order of sequences are highly significant. Montag is no longer a man instantly aware, immediately in revolt.

Clear issues are transformed into atmosphere and vague oppressions. During the first scene of "Fireman," the radio blares: war may be declared any minute. Now there is no mention, although planes are constantly in the sky. To create mood, the role of the Mechanical Hound is expanded. In the novella, it appears only during the chase. Now it is present from the start. It is in a niche at the firehouse; as Montag passes it stirs—later it will haunt and harry him. The Hound becomes his guilt and nemesis. Montag's fall plunges deep into some unconscious past. Those other books behind the grate were taken before: to what end? Only now does he begin to explore their meaning. He will not grasp it at all until the very iast. Captain Beatty has long suspected something, and tuned the Hound to him. Like the war that frames it, the drama that now surfaces is something long stirring in the depths of things. In "Fireman," Montag is made too immediately aware (Clarisse shows him the rain: "Why, it's *wine*!"), too critical for a man in his situation—a fireman emerging from cultural night.

And the issues are also too clear in this tale. In *Fahrenheit*, they purposely become opaque: either the figures are not aware of them, or their complexities of character make words and actions ambiguous. The earlier Millie had a stand—books are for "professors and radicals." In the novel, she has become a zombie, befuddled and forlorn, less a mouthpiece for reactionary ideas than a slave to her "parlor" of illusion. In "Fireman," the Captain is simply the enemy, a servant of law and order. Beatty, however, is a complex, twisted being—a scourge of books who speaks exclusively in quotes. His cat and mouse game, Montag realizes, is suicidal—"Beatty had wanted to die!" Faber's role too is altered. his meeting with Montag, in "Fireman," was merely the excuse for discussion. The hero wants to start a "revolution," to plant books in firemen's houses all across the nation. Faber tells him this is folly—the whole civilization has to fall before anything can be done. This is a key idea in *Fahrenheit*. But it is not said outright; rather it is implied in the futile gropings of the characters, men who hardly understand their own motivations, let alone have any clear social purpose When Montag, later, does plant one book, it is a hopeless gesture. Faber is both afraid and ineffectual. Out of their meeting comes no revolutionary plan, only human contact. Bradbury adds another device here—the "seashell" radio. Montag has not asked Faber to help him, as much as "to teach him." Now a guiding voice goes with him. This too is ineffectual; over Faber's admonitions, Montag explodes, and recites poetry to his wife's friends, betraying himself. But two beings are linked: in this fragmented world, it is a start.

Changes in the final scene help reshape *Fahrenheit*. The crucial moment is the rebirth, in Montag's mind, of *Ecclesiastes*. He had tried to memorize it before, and had despaired. Now, as the city falls, as he holds to the earth "as children do," it floods back. Earlier, he had plunged into the dark river, emerging into real nature: the fire of the sun, rather than man's perverted fire. The Mechanical Hound is replaced by a deer. But nature's darkness is also overwhelming. His dream of the hayloft—"a glass of milk, an apple, a pear"—is drowned in immensity: "Too much land!" He is saved by the campfire—flame that warms not burns. Once more, as with Faber, the paltry spark of human companionship is the merest beginning. In "Fireman" there is no evocation of nature, and little of this complex fire imagery. Montag's final triumph is sapped when characters discuss the faculty of "eidetic" memory. He tries to recall the Bible and can't; he is told to relax—"it will come when you need it." Bradbury shapes this rough skeleton into an extended statement of lyrical force. Indeed, if the early story seeks to expose, *Fahrenheit* mourns—the didactic tale has become elegy. Again there is the confused seeker after knowledge, again we see a world where excessive tolerance ironically leads to suppression of inquiry. The individual is powerless before the holocaust. Like the boy in "The Smile," he can only snatch away a fragment to preserve. Thought destroys, but memory abides. These last men do not interpret their books. Out of some strange fear of the old sin of pride, they are reduced to being the books, memorizing them one by one, and reciting them when needed. The tradition of oral history has come full circle.

DANDELION WINE & THE MARTIAN CHRONICLES

Both *Wine* and *Chronicles* are works composed of short tales and sketches Bradbury wrote at different times, on various occasions. In both cases, the material is skillfully assembled. *Chronicles*, however, is his masterpiece of lyrical organization: themes, tones, and variations, in length and mood are woven into a subtle pattern of resonances—counterpoint and contrast that are musical in nature. The two works are, in subject and technique, descendants of Anderson's *Winesburg, Ohio*. *Chronicles*, though the earlier of the two, is the more original and inventive in its adaptation of frame to stories.

Anderson threads his various lives together by the constant presence of young George Willard, a reporter for the *Winesburg Eagle*. Willard touches some of the lives incidentally, observing others, participating in still more; he is, however, marked by all. In the end, he goes away: life in town becomes "but a background on which to paint the dreams of his manhood." We are poised in curious ambiguity: adult life is to be a "dream," yet this adolescence remains "but a background." *Wine* has no openendedness at all. It begins with the first day of Summer 1928, and ends with the last—it is one marvelously rounded whole, its magic conserved in the numbered bottles of dandelion wine stored for winters to come. Within its compass, young Douglas Spaulding only seems to come of age: his first awareness of life is balanced by premonitions of death. Here is a complete existence in microcosmic potential, which expands outward to touch upon various town lives, only to contract back on itself. This is not Anderson's string of twisted apples. The boy is not so much shaped by these strange destinies, as they are absorbed and preserved in his memory—a different kind of vintage. In the short bridge passages that join the longer episodes, the principal actor assumes an odd choric function. Douglas sharpens his pencils, records, fixes, stores away each experience for future memory. In his late fever dream, Douglas sees all these lives pass again before the mind's eye: they are resumed and encapsulated by this one boy's existence. His final act is to stand in the cupola high above this town on the verge of autumn, moving his arms like an orchestra leader, and putting it to sleep. Whether he directs it, or it directs him, is irrelevant. He is now one with his world.

Anderson keeps a delicate balance between town and individual. *Wine* shifts emphasis to the one life at the center. *Chronicles* moves in the opposite direction. The bridge passages which encompass and unite the tales of single lives now reflect a collective presence—the voice of mankind in general. Bradbury's larger world is hardly universal in any real sense: Martian and Earthman alike shrink to the small town Midwesterner, if not in shape, than at least in mentality. Another change is more important. In *Chronicles*, these bridges lose their choric autonomy. Instead of commenting on individual actions, they provide lyrical contrast and thematic counterpoint. The individual and the collective voices blend, interacting here in a way found nowhere else in Bradbury.

Chronicles passes from Earth to Mars, from the unnatural "rocket summer," to a new summer in autumn where man finally must face the consequences of his actions. As the initial rocket takes off, it "blows clouds of fire and heat.'' Willingly or unwillingly, that same fire destroys both Mars and Earth. Ultimately, it drives a surviving family on its ''million-year picnic'' to an empty Red Planet. If we come full circle, it is only in the most mitigated sense. False summer becomes a real one, but here is another lame Bradbury phoenix, born of bleak October, 2026, and the near death of the race of man. But fire is now seen anew: the unnatural force has consumed itself, cleansed away the unnatural. The key to this new summer is acceptance—why not a ''picnic?'' The father burns all that is left of Earth. When the children ask: where are the Martians? he shows them their own reflections in the waters of their new home.

Throughout *Chronicles*, the identity of the Martians will be a problem. This question is linked with others: ''The men of Mars realized that in order to survive they would have to forgo asking that one question any longer: *Why live?* Life was its own answer..The Martians realized that they had asked the question: Why live at all? at the height of some period of war..when there was no answer. But once the civilization calmed, quieted...the question became senseless in a new way. Life now was good and needed no arguments.'' The reply is that they were ''naive.'' In terms of the dynamics of these *Chronicles*, perhaps they were, for change is the one constant.

The world of the first long episode ''Ylla'' is this same ''calmed, quieted'' civilization. But the seas are drying up, the culture is old and ingrown. People lead monotonous lonely lives. Into this world comes man. What really tears it asunder, however, is a fatal ''dream.'' The young Martian woman Ylla, in her yearning, makes telepathic contact with the leader of the first Earth Expedition. The fall is re-enacted. Through this breach alien images—strange song and new words—erupt into her life as it re-awakens to love. Provoked to jealousy, her husband kills Captain York. But this avails nothing: the rift is made, and it widens by itself. In the bridge passage, the whole planet begins to sing unknown songs. The second Expedition is rejected in a different way: the Martians refuse to see them, considering them ''madmen.'' Martians can project hallucinations with their minds; their psychotics abuse this. ''How natural if normal Martians think *we* produce our rocket ship with *our* minds.'' The psychiatrist shoots them, but the ''hallucinations'' persist. He believes he is ''contaminated,'' and kills himself. There is contamination, however. Where the creation of illusion was once insanity, with the Third Expedition it becomes deceit, a weapon.

Earthmen are maliciously trapped by the projections of their own desires and wants—Mars becomes "heaven." To resist the breach is only to make it wider. We pass from individual jealousy to scientific curiosity to collective guile. The Martians are corrupted long before the chickenpox strikes.

As the Martians fall, the Earthmen rise. But they too are blighted in the seed. In "Rocket Summer," technology casts its fatal shadow across their actions. Atom war is already in the air in another short sketch, "The Taxpayer." This man would make the wrong move for the right reasons. He is against war and censorship. But he would run off to Mars rather than face the problem, accepting responsibility for his actions. As man runs, the rift widens. It is immediately visible in the first episode of Earthmen on Mars, "And the Moon Be Still as Bright." War errupts between these "rugged individualists," the spoilers, and the archeologist Spender, who is drawn to the old planet: "They never let science crush the aesthetic and the beautiful." What has gone before casts an ironic shadow over Spender's actions. "Good" intentions lead to armed violence and death. The new frontier is defiled from the first.

Yet the process of colonization goes through. It is dominated, however, by an alternating rhythm: progress or blight, Earth future or Martian past. The first settlers come—the "lonely ones." In "Green Morning," a new Johnny Appleseed plants trees on Mars—man needs to have air. A green planet springs up in this "alien and magical soil" overnight. But this acceleration brings the countering one of "The Locusts." "And from the rockets ran men with hammers in their hands to beat the strange world into a shape that was familiar to the eye."

At the center of the *Chronicles* there is a strange moment of balance, and stasis. In "Night Meeting," an Earthman meets a Martian on the road. Both are going somewhere, but neither will admit the other's existence. They cannot touch, but the fact they see and talk to each other contaminates. "Ruins, you say?" The Martian suddenly sees himself as past. But what wil the future bring to the Earthman: "Who wants to see the future?" Here is a privileged moment: "What does it matter who is past or future, if we are both alive?" But it is unstable. Caught in the pull of time, such naive faith dissolves.

This point of suspension coincides with the arrival of the second, middle wave of settlers. After the frontiersmen come the city dwellers—the poor and the sophisticates alike. Two tales balance. In "Way in the

Middle of the Air," the Negroes leave the South in rockets for Mars. "Usher II tells of the advent of the rule and regulation makers. The rush to freedom is offset by this new slavery. But at the same time, there is a forward thrust; in each tale, fantasy triumphs. On this plane too there is a cancelling. The Blacks excape their mockers and tormentors in rocket ships like "sweet chariots." William Stendhal, however rids himself of his tormentors by murdering them in his mechanized horror chamber. This oscillating rhythm is condensed in the bridge passage, "The Musicians." The boys' games with old Martian bones contrast with the antiseptic activity of the "firemen," who would clean up the planet. The sketch prefaces these alternating tales; and yet it gives the impetus that will ultimately carry things forward. The fireman will win out. Life is offset by death, Mars and Usher swallow the Blacks, fantasy is purged by the forces of "reason," who in turn burn one death only to create another.

The third wave arrives—the "old ones." In "The Martian," reason gives way before the need for illusion. An old couple comes to Mars to escape their past on Earth—their dead son. They find and lose him again on Mars. This Martian is the opposite of earlier ones. Ylla's yearning drew York; Martians harnessed the dreams of the Third Expedition to destroy it. The pathetic figure here is "trapped" by the psychic needs of several lonely and forlorn men—not only is he torn asunder, but, in a counterblow, the dreamers are crushed as well. This is a private mirror for the atom war that is now rending Earth, thereby destroying the new Mars. With logic that echoes that of the earlier "taxpayer," men rush home: "I know we came up here to get away from things—politics, the atom bomb, war...But it's still home there." In "The Off Season," Parkhill one of the original spoilers of Mars, is in turn spoiled by Earth. Just as his hot-dog stand is ready for business, war erupts; it will always be an offseason. Ironically, the Martian ghosts return to give him a land grant to half this empty planet.

In three final tales, the death of this new Mars is mirrored by that of Earth. In "The Silent Towns," a lone man at last places a phone call—a woman is alive. But when he finally sees her, she is so monstrous that he flees. Solitude is better than this. "The Long Years" contrasts with this humorous affirmation of loneliness. Hathaway of the old Fourth Expedition, Spender's group, returns. He has suffered so much from the death of wife and family, from the silence of the towns, that he peoples them with mechanical noises, builds a robot family to replace the other. When Hathaway dies, the robots remain, performing their domestic tasks in the void. In mirror fashion, in "There Will Come Soft Rains," a mechanical house on Earth continues to function though its owners are dead and the city bombed. Now, however, we witness the agony of this house, the last testament to man's folly and marvelous fantasy.

But out of this despair comes unexpected hope. The mechanical dies reciting the Teasdale poem in a human voice. The soft rains of radioactive death will also be those of rebirth. Thus, in the last tale, a mechanical rocket takes its family to Mars—it is a "silver seed." The bridges are finally cut, the map of Earth is burned, the rhythm of alternation not more. In "Dark They Were," Mars changed the Earth-men's bodies and minds, made them different and more beautiful. Nothing of that sort happens here. Men remain men; if the things of Earth are destroyed, the memory of their folly remains. The world has changed around them. And they can only accept.

CONCLUSION

Has Bradbury passed his peak as writer? His great works are surely the earlier ones. And his last really original creation to date is probably "I Sing." Of the tales included in his most recent collection, *Long After Midnight*, some are old, and the new ones offer very little that is new. The plays and poetry he has been writing lately are not particularly good. But all this should not detract from his very real accomplishments as a writer. Bradbury has been unjustly neglected by the critics, and this study awakens some new interest in his work. Uncovering the pattern of meaning is most important in dealing with Bradbury's work. This "dark" view of the writer may prove surprising. Through it, however, Ray Bradbury joins a deep current in American thought and letters.

RAY DOUGLAS BRADBURY was born August 22, 1920, at Waukegan, Illinois. His father, Leonard Bradbury, was an electrical lineman by profession; his mother was a native-born Swede. Bradbury sold newspapers on a Los Angeles street corner for three years (1939-42), when his income from writing short stories ($20 a week) enabled him to quit, and devote full time to writing. His first published story, "It's Not the Heat It's the Hu--", appeared in *Rob Wagner's Script Magazine* on November 2, 1940. Bradbury won a Benjamin Franklin Award for best short story published in a popular magazine during 1953, and was the recipient of an American Academy of Arts and Letters $1,000 award for his contributions to American literature (1954). Ray Bradbury lives in Los Angeles with his wife and four daughters. A list of his published books follows:

BIBLIOGRAPHY

1. *Dark Carnival.* Arkham House, Sauk City, 1947, 313p, Cloth, Coll.
2. *The Martian Chronicles.* Doubleday, Garden City, 1950, 222p, Cloth, Coll.
2A. retitled: *The Silver Locusts.* Rupert Hart-Davis, London, 1951, 232p, Cloth, Coll. [Drops one story, adds one story]
3. *The Illustrated Man.* Doubleday, Garden City, 1951, 252p, Cloth, Coll.
4. *Timeless Stories for Today and Tomorrow.* Bantam, New York, 1952, 306p, Paper, Anth.
5. *The Golden Apples of the Sun.* Doubleday, Garden City, 1953, 250p, Cloth, Coll.
6. *Fahrenheit 451.* Ballantine, New York, 1953, 201p, Cloth, Coll.
7. *Fahrenheit 451.* Rupert Hart-Davis, London, 1954, 158p, Cloth, Novel.
8. *Switch on the Night.* Pantheon, New York, 1955, 52p, Cloth, Juvn.
9. *The October Country.* Ballantine, New York, 1955, 306p, Paper, Coll.
10. *The Circus of Dr. Lao, and Other Improbable Stories.* Bantam, New York, 1956, 210p, Paper, Anth.
11. *Sun and Shadow.* Quenian Press, Berkeley, 1957, 19p, Cloth, Story
12. *Dandelion Wine.* Doubleday, Garden City, 1957, 281p, Cloth, Coll.

13. *A Medicine for Melancholy*. Doubleday, Garden City, 1959, 240p, Cloth, Coll.
14. *The Day It Rained Forever*. Rupert Hart-Davis, London, 1959, 254p, Cloth, Coll.
15. *Something Wicked This Way Comes*. Simon & Schuster, New York, 1962, 317p, Cloth, Novel.
16. *The Small Assassin*. Ace Books, London, 1962, 144p, Paper, Coll.
17. *R Is for Rocket*. Doubleday, Garden City, 1962, 233p, Cloth, Coll.
18. *The Anthem Sprinters, and Other Antics*. Dial Press, New York, 1963, 159p, Cloth, Play Coll.
19. *The Machineries of Joy; Short Stories*. Simon & Schuster, New York, 1964, 255p, Cloth, Coll.
20. *The Pedestrian*. Roy Squires, Glendale, 1964, 16p, Paper, Story
21. *The Vintage Bradbury; Ray Bradbury's Own Selection of His Best Stories*. Vintage Books, New York, 1965, 331p, Paper, Coll.
22. *Twice Twenty-Two; The Golden Apples of the Sun; A Medicine for Melancholy*. Doubleday, Garden City, 1966, 406p, Cloth, Coll.
23. *The Day It Rained Forever*. Samuel French, New York, 1966, 24p, Paper, Play
24. *The Pedestrian*. Samuel French, New York, 1966, 22p, Paper, Play
25. *S Is for Space*. Doubleday, Garden City, 1966, 238p, Cloth, Coll.
26. *I Sing the Body Electric! Stories*. Alfred A. Knopf, New York, 1969, 305p, Cloth, Coll.
27. *Old Ahab's Friend, and Friend to Noah, Speaks His Piece; A Celebration*. Roy Squires, Glendale, 1971, 16p, Paper, Poem.
28. *The Wonderful Ice Cream Suit, and Other Plays*. Bantam Pathfinder Editions, New York, 1972, 161p, Paper, Play Coll.
29. *Madrigals for the Space Age, for Mixed Chorus and Narrator with Piano Accompaniment*. Associated Music Publishers, New York, 1972, 43p, Paper, Music
30. *The Halloween Tree*. Alfred A. Knopf, New York, 1972, 145p, Cloth, Juvn.
31. *Zen and the Art of Writing; and, The Joy of Writing; Two Essays*. Capra Press, Santa Barbara, 1973, 24p, Cloth, Coll.
32. *When Elephants Last in the Dooryard Bloomed; Celebrations for Almost Any Day in the Year*. Alfred A. Knopf, New York, 1973, 143p, Cloth, Poetry Coll.
33. *Teacher's Guide; Science Fiction*. Bantam, New York, 1973?, 16p, Paper, Nonf. (with Lewy Olfson)

34. *Ray Bradbury*. George G. Harrap, London, 1975, 188p, Cloth, Coll.
35. *Pillar of Fire, and Other Plays for Today, Tomorrow, and Beyond Tomorrow*. Bantam, New York, 1975, 114p, Paper, Play Coll.
36. *That Ghost, That Bride of Time; Excerpts from a Play-in-Progress Based on the Moby Dick Mythology, and Dedicated to Herman Melville*. Bradbury, Los Angeles, 1976, 16p, Paper, Play
37. *Long After Midnight*. Alfred A. Knopf, New York, 1976, 271p, Cloth, Coll.